Greenland Right Whale

Biscayan Right Whale

Antarctic Bottlenose Whale

Minke Whale

Sei Whale

Humpback Whale

Pigmy Sperm Whale

Arctic Bottlenose Whale

The Life and Death of Whales

The Life and Death of Whales

Robert Burton

UNIVERSE BOOKS
New York

Published in the United States of America in 1973
by Universe Books, 381 Park Avenue South, New York, N.Y. 10016

Copyright © 1973 by Robert Burton

Second printing, 1973
Third printing, 1975

Library of Congress Catalog Card Number: 72-95463

ISBN 0-87663-183-9

Printed in Great Britain

Contents

List of illustrations

Tables

Acknowledgements

Many writers have set down their experience of whales or whaling, or have gathered together obscure or scattered observations. This book draws together a sample of the immense stock of information that exists. Like similar books it cannot cover the whole and it relies heavily on published works by authors who have already shed light on the habits of whales and their pursuit by man. I am indebted to these authors, and also to Nigel Bonner who gave me the benefit of his knowledge.

Part I

The Life of Whales

God seems to have made the whale as a proof of his power. It is in every respect the finest animal in nature. Whatever care we take to imagine a large animal beforehand, yet the first sight of this huge creature never fails to strike us with astonishment and awe. Having been used to smaller animals, we have no conception of its enormous magnitude: for a moving column of flesh 102 feet long and 75 feet in circumference is an object so utterly different from those we are constantly presented with, that, to be comprehended, it must actually be seen: but the skeleton of the whale is by far a finer subject of curiosity than the whale itself; the whale, at first view, presents the spectator with an enormous mass of flesh, and scarcely seems animated, until pursued by the swordfish, or struck by the harpooner. When, however, the mass of flesh is removed, and the skeleton stands confessed and exposed, as it now does in Gloucester Green, it is then that we acknowledge that 'those who go down to the sea in ships see the wonders of the deep', and that there is no mechanical structure to be compared with the skeleton of the whale.

When the illustrious Galen examined a similar skeleton, he suddenly became converted from the errors of Atheism. Who can contemplate this mighty skeleton, without adoring the Mind that formed it? Where can we better cultivate a sentiment of devotion than in the presence of a work so expressive of the various attributes of the varied God?

From a nineteenth-century handbill advertising the exhibition of a whale skeleton

1. Whales Defined and Described

The whales belong to the mammalian order of *Cetacea*, a group of animals which includes the large whales, such as the blue, fin and sperm whales, smaller whales, such as the killer and pilot whales, and various porpoises and dolphins. All live in water and all have roughly the same shape: a stream-lined, fish-shaped body with flippers and flukes for propulsion. Many of them have been hunted, mainly for their blubber which is rendered down to oil, and for their meat. Hunting of the larger whales has developed into an important industry yet, because of their inaccessibility, less is known about their lives than those of their small relatives, the porpoises and dolphins. Porpoises and dolphins are going to be largely ignored in this book while an attempt is made to set forth the lives of the large whales using what information has been gleaned from observations at sea and the studies of their anatomy. The whaling industry has provided both opportunity and need for these studies and its history makes up the second half of the book.

Whales are familiar animals. They are as much a part of our general know-ledge as lions and tigers and elephants and hippopotamuses. Yet an accurate definition of whales has proved a problem to zoologists and laymen alike for centuries, and it is still not properly resolved. When men started to name and classify animals they grouped them on the basis of external appearance and so made many mistakes about true relationships. The whales were classed as fishes by mediaeval scholars, because they lived in the sea and had fins but no fur. Such a classification had a very practical use as it meant that whale flesh could be eaten during Lent. The development of a 'natural' system of classification came slowly and culminated in the scheme, worked out by the Swedish naturalist Linnaeus in the eighteenth century, which has been used ever since. Linnaeus classed whales as mammals, a term that was first coined by him in 1773 to cover the four-footed, furry animals, then known loosely as beasts, and their less obvious relatives such as bats and whales. The name only came into popular use about fifty years later.

The whales are classed as mammals because they have features common to other mammals. They are warm-blooded, they breathe air, they bear their young alive and suckle them and they even have traces of hair. To think of them as fishes, cold-blooded, breathing with gills and covered with scales, now seems ridiculous, as Aristotle realized in the fourth century BC. His wisdom was ignored for centuries and whales were defined as fish because they lived in the sea, had streamlined bodies and swam by means of fins.

If one agrees with this definition, a whale is undoubtedly a fish and even Herman Melville, the author of *Moby Dick*, pronounced that 'a whale is a spouting fish with a horizontal tail'. It is not a scientific definition, but it is only in recent years that people outside the small band of specialists have been expected to think about animals in scientific terms. As far as whalers were concerned, their quarry were 'fish' and they talked of 'fishing grounds' and 'fisheries'. (When searching for books on whaling it is even advisable to pay attention to those shelves devoted to works on angling.) This is fair enough for those employed in killing whales, where 'fish' is a technical term used by the profession, but it is a bad starting point for discussion of the biology of whales, where an understanding of the whale's place in the animal kingdom is essential.

Our understanding of the relationships of animals and their proper position in the evolutionary scale has come from the study of anatomy, or body structure, in which we can see that closely related animals have similar bodies, particularly in the form of the skeleton. Study of the skeleton is particularly important because the skeletons of extinct animals have survived as fossils, and through their study it is possible to find animals that are common ancestors to different species alive today.

The search for an ancestor of the whales and a clue to their relationship to other mammals has proved difficult. They are so well adapted for life in the sea, with the all-important skeleton being modified for swimming rather than walking, that it is not possible even to point to a distant land living relative. A study of the fossil record is often useful in tracing relationships that have been obscured by change; but all the fossils of whales that have been unearthed are of animals that are already proper whales, and show no trace of features that would link them with a land living ancestor. We can only assume, therefore, that whales branched very early from the 'trunk' of the mammalian evolutionary tree. All we have is a little evidence that whales may be related to the cloven-hoofed mammals, such as cattle, deer and antelopes.

When a whale is examined in detail the enormous changes that have taken place to transform it from a land to a marine animal become clear. Its shape, its skeleton, its means of propulsion, the workings of the respiratory system and the sense organs have undergone profound changes. At first sight they would appear to be quite unrelated to the equivalent parts of a land mammal but they are based on the same plan. There has been a programme of modification rather than of replacement in the evolution of the whales; except in the organs of propulsion where the limbs of a land mammal have been replaced by a fluked tail. These changes are described in later chapters, but the basic form of a whale must be understood and the different kinds of whales described before making any detailed examination of their lives and habits.

The striking feature of whales, when compared to any other group of mammals, is their extreme size. Life in the sea, with the body supported on all sides by a cushion of water, releases them from the restraints that gravity imposes on land animals: no set of limbs of a conventional form could support the body of a whale sized land animal. The actual size of a large whale is not easy to comprehend. A few blue whales, the largest species, have been found to measure over a hundred feet and a rough guide for a whale's weight is one ton for one foot of length. These animals can be equated with a herd of elephants or 1,500 men, but such comparisons do not readily convey an impression of the bulk of such a creature. A better way of appreciating their size is to walk round the model of the blue whale displayed in the British Museum (Natural History) and imagine rowing in a small boat alongside such an animal. It is no wonder that the writer of the handbill quoted at the head of this part of the book should expound so eloquently on the size of his exhibit and to consider that it was a practical lesson in divinity.

An even more evocative account of the size of these animals is that of a dissection of a stranded whale as described by Francis Buckland:

> He [the dissector] carefully descended into the gigantic mass of anatomical horrors, and took out what parts he wanted. This service was not, however, done without danger, for when dissecting the enormous heart his foot slipped, and he fell into one of the cavities of the heart, his feet passing down into the great artery, the aorta. Assistance was luckily at hand, or he might have met with a fatal accident. To show the narrow escape he had, he subsequently cut rings out of this aorta, and found that he could pass them, without stretching, over his head and shoulders right down to his feet.

A large part of the whale's bulk is composed of a thick layer of blubber which keeps the body warm, acts as a food reserve and gives the whale its streamlined appearance. The head is large and almost free of blubber which becomes very thick just behind the head so that it disguises the short neck and smooths out the line of the body. The shape of the head is distinctly odd when compared with that of the head of a horse or a dog. Nostrils at the tip of the muzzle have been replaced by a 'blowhole' on top of the head, the eyes are set well down the sides of the head and the mouth has a long, grinning gape. At first sight it seems as if the breathing passages must connect with the blowhole through the middle of the brain, but the head has not been so drastically reorganized. There has merely been a reshaping of the skull, some parts being enlarged and others being reduced. The effect has been to shorten the muzzle (the nasal bone) so that the nostrils are close

Figure 1 Skulls of (a) a horse and (b) a whalebone whale, to show the changes undergone by whales. ■ – nasal bone, ▨ – premaxilla, N – nostril or blowhole.

against the braincase (Figure 1). At the same time the bone forming the upper lip (the premaxilla) is greatly enlarged to form a secondary muzzle or 'beak' in which there are rows of teeth or whalebone plates.

The streamlining of a whale is broken by as few obstructions as on a jet aeroplane. There is a pair of flippers behind the head, a pair of flukes on the tail and in many species there is a fin in the middle of the back. The flippers are the last visible remains of the two pairs of limbs owned by the whale's unknown land ancestor. From the arm or leg of a land animal the whale's forelimb has become shortened and flattened to make a broad paddle. The arm bones – the humerus, radius and ulna – are very short and the fingers are joined in a common bag of skin. There are five fingers in each flipper, the same number as in the basic mammalian hand or foot, but three of the fingers are very long. All movement of the arm and hand joints is lost and the flipper has become a rigid structure that can bend only at the shoulder joint.

A rudimentary hindlimb appears in an embryo whale but it disappears long before the whale is born. All that is left of the hindlimbs and the pelvic girdle is one or two bones on each side of the body. They are not attached to the backbone as in most mammals but are buried in a mass of muscle. In males, these bones form an anchor for the penis. The role of locomotion has been taken over from the limbs by the tail which is thick and powerful, as in fishes. The tip of the tail is drawn out into two flat flukes which act as propellor blades. They are set horizontally and beat up and down, in contrast to those of fishes which are vertical and swing from side to side.

The description given above is of a generalized, anonymous whale, but there are many species of whale and they vary considerably in appearance and habits. There is also some confusion about what species can be properly called whales, as distinct from porpoises and dolphins. This has happened because the names of these animals arose centuries before zoologists started to classify animals. It was quite easy to define whales as mammals and not fish but there is still no agreement as to which of the species should be classed as true whales.

Linnaeus grouped the whales, porpoises and dolphins in the order *Cetacea* and sometimes the whole order is called 'the whales' for convenience. In

2

		Probable maximum length (feet)	Distribution
ORDER *Cetacea*			
SUBORDER *Mysticeti* (whalebone or baleen whales)			
FAMILY *Balaenidae*			
Greenland right whale or bowhead (*Balaena mysticetus*)		60	Arctic seas
Biscayan or black right whale (*Eubalaena glacialis*)	ca	60	Cosmopolitan except tropics
Pigmy right whale (*Caperea marginata*)	ca	20	Antarctic seas
FAMILY *Eschrichtiidae*			
Gray whale (*Eschrichtius gibbosus*)	ca	45	North Pacific
FAMILY *Balaenopteridae* (rorquals)			
Blue whale (*Balaenoptera musculus*)		107	Cosmopolitan
Fin whale (*B. physalus*)		85	Cosmopolitan
Sei whale (*B. borealis*)		60	Cosmopolitan
Bryde's whale (*B. brydei*)	ca	50	Warmer seas
Minke whale (*B. acutorostrata*)	ca	32	Cosmopolitan
Humpback whale (*Megaptera novae-angliae*)		50	Cosmopolitan
SUBORDER *Odontoceti* (toothed whales)			
FAMILY *Physeteridae*			
Sperm whale (*Physeter macrocephalus*) male		60	Cosmopolitan
female		40	
Pigmy sperm whale (*Kogia breviceps*)	ca	13	Cosmopolitan
FAMILY *Ziphiidae* (beaked whales)			
Baird's beaked whale (*Berardius bairdii*)		42	North Pacific
Arctic bottlenose whale (*Hyperoodon ampullatus*)	ca	30	Arctic seas
Antarctic bottlenose whale (*H. planifrons*)		30	Antarctic seas
FAMILY *Delphinidae* (dolphins)			
Pilot whale (*Globicephala melaena*)	ca	22	Cosmopolitan
Killer whale (*Orcinus orca*)		33	Cosmopolitan

Table I. Species, their size and distribution. Few specimens of whales have been measured in relation to the numbers caught, so greater maximum lengths are possible, especially in little known species. Average lengths of whales caught are much less, about twenty feet, for the blue whale.

popular language, however, the term 'whale' is usually reserved for the larger members of the order, but where the boundary is to be drawn is largely a matter of personal preference. One writer may decide that a length of over twenty feet is the qualification of a whale and another may decide on thirty feet or more, but there is always the awkward situation caused by the killer whale, which sometimes tops thirty feet, being a member of the dolphin family; while the pigmy sperm whale, which is a close relative of the giant sperm whale, reaches only thirteen feet in length. Perhaps it is best to describe whales as the 'larger cetaceans' and this vague term covers the animals that form the subject of this book. It is a purely arbitrary distinction which covers the species that make up the basis of the major whaling industries but which excludes the numerous porpoises and dolphins.

The order *Cetacea* is divided into two very distinctive groups, both of which include whales as they are defined above. Most of the true whales are in the suborder *Mysticeti*, the whalebone or baleen whales. These are the whales that feed mainly on small animals which they sieve from the sea by means of rows of whalebone or baleen plates hanging from the upper jaw. They have no teeth except in the developing embryo. To accommodate the baleen the head is very large and the lower jaw is a little longer than the upper.

With the exception of the sperm whale, the whalebone whales have been the whales most sought after by hunters. They are divided into three families.

All members of the family *Balaenidae* are now rare. They are the right whales, so-called because they were the right whales for the whalers to catch from open boats. They swam slowly, floated when dead and yielded large quantities of valuable whalebone. The Biscayan or black right whale became scarce many years ago. It is found in all temperate and subpolar seas and the southern form, the southern right whale, is sometimes classed as a separate species. The Greenland right whale or bowhead is confined to Arctic seas.

The right whales are the most distinctive of all whalebone whales. The head takes up one third of the body length. The upper jaw is arched and the lips of the lower jaw rise each side to enclose the numerous baleen plates which grow up to twelve feet long. The Biscayan right whale bears a peculiar structure of tough, roughened skin on the snout. This is called the bonnet and has no known function. The bonnet and similar outgrowths are infested with the whale louse, an amphipod crustacean, which lives in the crevices of the horny skin on which it feeds. A similar whale louse lives on the head and flippers of the bowhead.

The pigmy right whale is one of the rarest of whales. It is known almost entirely from specimens stranded on the shores of southern seas and grows to about twenty feet, one third the size of the other right whales. It differs from them in the possession of a dorsal fin.

The right whales are now so rare that they are hardly ever seen. There is a small population of bowheads in the North Pacific; but only odd individuals or very small groups of the Biscayan species are seen and if the species is recovering, the increase is very slow.

Prospects are much more encouraging for the gray whale, the sole member of the family *Eschrichtiidae*. This whale lives on both sides of the North Pacific and was killed in large numbers by the whalers of the nineteenth century. Under strict protection the population has recovered to some extent, and its habit of migrating close to the shores of California, which once made it easy to hunt, has now made it a tourist attraction. There is considerable evidence that gray whales lived and were hunted in the North Atlantic during historical times (see Chapter 8). The gray whale grows to about forty-five feet. Like the right whales it has no dorsal fin but it has a row of knobs on the back and two or four grooves on the throat, similar to those found on the third family, the *Balaenopteridae* or rorquals.

The name rorqual is derived from the old Norwegian *rörhval*, referring to the grooves that run from just behind the lower lip to the chest. There is a dorsal fin and the flippers are pointed rather than rounded as in the right whales. Rorquals are more streamlined than the right whales, with flatter heads and short baleen plates. There are six species and among them are the largest of the whales, which have formed the mainstay of the whaling industry throughout this century.

The largest of the rorquals is the blue whale, the largest animal which has ever existed. A few specimens have topped one hundred feet, and one captured in 1922 measured one hundred and seven feet. The weight of such animals is thought to be 130–150 tons, much depending on the amount of blubber. Naturally, such giants were eagerly sought by whalers and during the course of this century their numbers have been reduced from an estimated 30,000 to around 1,000. They are now protected and they seem to be recovering slightly. The blue whale was called the 'sulphur-bottom' by whalers because the blue-grey of its belly is sometimes coloured yellow by a film of diatoms.

Small mature blue whales have been caught from time to time in the Antarctic whaling grounds, particularly around the island of Kerguelen. Some whale authorities consider that these are a race or species of pigmy blue whale but others are more sceptical, and feel that this is an attempt to find an excuse to hunt members of a species that has been given complete protection from hunting.

The second largest rorqual is the fin whale which reaches about eighty-five feet. It is the most abundant of the large whales and became the main target of the whalers after the decline of the blue whale. Fin whales look like small, slender blue whales but have larger dorsal fins and white bellies. There is also a strange lopsided coloration of the head; the lower right lip and the anterior, right-hand baleen plates are white.

Smaller still is the sei (pronounced 'sigh') whale. *Sei* is the Norwegian for the coalfish, a relative of the cod, and the sei whale appears off the Norwegian coast at the same time each year as the fish. The sei whale looks like the fin whale, but only grows to about sixty feet and lacks the asymmetric colouring. Very similar is Bryde's (pronounced 'Breuder's) whale, which was only distinguished as a separate species in 1913 and is found only in warmer seas. It is recognized by broader baleen plates, longer ventral grooves which reach as far as the umbilicus and three parallel ridges on the snout. The smallest rorqual is the minke whale or lesser rorqual. It rarely exceeds thirty feet and is recognized by white baleen and a white band on the flippers. The lesser rorqual earned the name of minke whale when a Norwegian whaler, Miencke, mistook these diminutive rorquals for blue whales.

The last of the rorquals is the humpback whale. Its appearance is very different from the others. The body is stout and the flippers measure one third of the total length. Both head and flippers are covered with irregular knobs. The ventral grooves are deeper but fewer in number than in other rorquals. The humpback migrates close to the shore so that the routes taken are well known, but this habit also makes it easy to catch and the numbers of humpbacks have been severely reduced.

*

The second great group of whales forms the suborder *Odontoceti*, or toothed whales. It includes the sperm whale, the killer whale and numerous porpoises and dolphins, many of which are becoming familiar as performing animals in marine aquaria. The jaws of toothed whales are armed with peg teeth, rather like the incisors of a dog, which are used in the capture of fish and squid. The nostrils are combined into a single orifice and there is a rounded forehead, called the melon from the French for a bowler hat. The melon is filled with a fine oil which used to be very valuable as a lubricant. The skulls of odontocetes are most unusual in that they are not symmetrical, that is, the left and right hand sides are not equal. In some species this has led to the blowhole being on the left side of the head, but asymmetry is most marked in the narwhal where the tusk of the male is a very much enlarged tooth from the left-hand side of the jaw.

The sperm whale is the largest of the toothed whales and the most bizarre in appearance. The melon has been enlarged into an enormous, rounded snout of fibrous tissue. The upper part is known as the case and is filled with a clear liquid, called spermaceti, which sets to a wax when cool. Between the case and the jaw is a layer of fibrous fatty tissue, called junk by the whalers. The blowhole is at the tip of the snout, and to one side rather than on the top of the head. The dorsal fin is replaced by a low hump. Sperm whales were very important commercially in the eighteenth and nineteenth centuries and are becoming important again as the numbers of rorquals diminish.

Sperm whales dive to great depths in search of food, which includes giant squid. They live in schools consisting of males and females, or young males alone, but old males may be solitary. Males grow to twice the size of females, that is to about sixty feet. The most famous sperm whale is Moby Dick, a white 'rogue male'. Although a fictitious character, he was based on stories of rogue males who were well known to whalers. Albinos of sperm whales and other species have been known to exist and a fifty-five foot white sperm whale, complete with a crooked jaw like Moby Dick's, was caught in the Pacific in 1951.

The pigmy sperm whale rarely grows longer than twelve feet and looks more like a porpoise than its large relative. Very little is known about it.

Among the larger toothed whales are the beaked whales, some of which are extremely rare. Baird's beaked whale reaches forty-two feet and is hunted in the North Pacific; the two bottlenose whales, one found in the Arctic and the other in the Antarctic, grow up to thirty feet. They lack teeth completely, except in old males where one tooth erupts on each side of the lower jaw. The Arctic species is hunted.

Pilot whales or blackfish are twenty-foot dolphins that live in schools sometimes numbering hundreds. For centuries they have been caught by being driven ashore and stranded.

The killer whale is another large dolphin, distinguished by a white patch behind the eye and a tall dorsal fin which reaches six feet in old males. The blade-shaped fin led to its being given the confusing name of sword-fish (as in the extract from the handbill). Male killer whales sometimes grow to more than thirty feet, and it is often said that females only reach half this length but recent measurements indicate that, on average, females are only 1–2 foot shorter than the males. Killer whales live in small groups and feed mainly on fish but they also kill seals and other whales. They, in turn, are hunted, to protect fisheries, or for their meat and blubber.

2. The Study of Whales

During the Middle Ages, zoology became an armchair study. Animals and habits were described from previous accounts and from travellers' tales. Not surprisingly, some strange notions crept in, either through faulty recollection or misunderstanding, or through attempts to describe what the writer, often a cloistered monk, felt ought to be the way of things. One idea current during this period was that all land animals had their equivalent in the sea, so sea-horses, sea-cows and sealions were invented. It is more by good luck than anything else that suitable animals have been found to take these names (the original sea-horses were walruses, not the peculiar little fishes that now bear this name).

There were some strange ideas about whales, although at this time they were common around European coasts and not infrequently became stranded. Their large size, strange appearance and marine way of life had brought them into the folklore of the seafaring peoples of north-west Europe. Stranded whales were regarded as portents of great events, such as the outbreak of war, and there were good whales that helped with the fishing and bad whales that upset boats and ate men.

Aristotle had already described the main features of the whales' biology centuries previously, but his knowledge was ignored until the revival of learning that marked the end of the Middle Ages. Anatomists now took the trouble to dissect stranded specimens (and it was a trouble; witness Buckland's account of the fate that nearly befell an anatomist). Studies of whales at large were much rarer and until the twentieth century there were only two outstanding works devoted to the lives of whales. There was William Scoresby's *Account of the Arctic Regions, with a History and Description of the Northern Whale-fishery*, from which we obtain much of our knowledge of the Greenland right whale, and Charles Scammon's *The Marine Mammals of he*

North-western Coasts of North America, which has a very detailed account of the gray whale.

Apart from the whalers, who generally observed whales in a disturbed situation, to say the least, it was difficult for anyone to study the lives of whales because most of them live in very remote places and they spend much of their time underwater. However, with the great development of whaling in the twentieth century, when it became necessary to find out where the whales were and how they could best be exploited, Government sponsored research organizations were set up.

Modern whale research has followed two interrelated courses: the basic study of whale biology, and the assessment of the stocks of whales with a view to regulating the numbers caught. Neither task is simple because of the scale involved. Dissection of a gigantic whale carcase is not easy, particularly when it causes a delay in working of the whale factory, and information about the movements of whales and their food supply has to be gathered over a vast area of ocean. Only in recent years, as both large whales and the whaling industry appear to be nearing extinction, has it become possible to describe the basic biological facts of population size, growth rate and expectation of life.

The initiative for whale research came from Norway and Britain, originally the two most important whaling countries. Pioneer work was started before World War I and was resumed on a large scale afterwards. Emphasis was placed very definitely on the Antarctic populations of whales because they formed the major part of the world's catch. Thus any discussion of whales, their reproduction, feeding or migration, or of whaling, its success or control, is biased towards the Antarctic and it is quite easy to get the impression that whales and whaling are confined to Antarctic seas. Both are cosmopolitan.

In Norway, whale research took the form of the collection of data from the whaling industry. The Norwegian Whaling Association gathered information about each whale caught; its species, sex, length and the region in which it was caught. This work still continues and the data are published in the *International Whaling Statistics*. Analyses of these figures have given important information about the distribution of whales and their populations.

British research work was directed at the whales themselves, as zoologists were stationed at the whaling factories where they could examine and dissect the whale carcases as they were brought in. The work was directed by the Discovery Committee, a body set up in 1924 to investigate the biology and oceanography of the Falkland Island Dependencies, a large slice of the Southern Ocean and South Atlantic which then enclosed the main Antarctic whaling grounds. The Discovery Committee's work was focused on whale biology but the cruises of the *Discovery*, Captain Scott's old expedition ship, and later the *Discovery II* were also concerned with other aspects of Antarctic biology and oceanography. With the expansion of the whaling industry to cover all the Southern Ocean, the cruises of the *Discovery II* were extended around the Antarctic continent and the Southern Ocean became the most thoroughly studied of all oceans.

Observations from the *Discovery* cruises made it possible to plot the distribution of the whales around the Antarctic, and to show that concentrations of whales coincided with regions of abundant plankton, the minute floating life of the sea, and that these, in turn, were correlated with the movement of ocean currents. This information is of great importance to the whalers who can attempt to forecast the whereabouts of plentiful whales by examination of water temperatures, currents and plankton concentrations.

While the *Discovery* cruises were in progress, other zoologists examined over 1,600 whale carcases brought in to whaling factories. Their work formed the basis of much of subsequent whale research. They were able to gather information on the growth and reproduction of whales that was not available from the figures given to the Norwegian statisticians. By examination of their reproductive state throughout the year, the mating season, and period of gestation and suckling were worked out, and examination of scars on the ovaries gave an indication of the numbers of calves that had been born to each whale.

The extension of this work was to find out the rate of growth, the age of puberty and life expectancy. Such information is essential for working out the structure of the population (the numbers of animals of various ages) and the rate at which new individuals are added to it through breeding. From this it is possible to calculate the rate at which animals can be removed from a population without a serious decrease in numbers. As it was apparent that whaling was causing a decline in the whale populations, it became very important to calculate the breeding rates of the various whale species, so that limits could be placed on the numbers caught. This was impossible until a method of determining the age of a whale had been discovered, so that the information about its reproductive state could be put into perspective.

To determine the age of an animal it is necessary to find some physiological feature that varies with age in a regular fashion. Length is an obvious choice, but mammals stop growing after they are physically mature and the rate of growth varies between individuals. This is obvious in human populations. It is impossible to guess an adult's age by his height. What was needed was some feature of the whale that continued growing after maturity and showed a seasonal change in the rate of growth. In other words, the search was for the equivalent of the annual rings in the trunk of a tree, where each ring represents a season's growth followed by a period of dormancy. The rorqual whales have an annual cycle in behaviour, in that they feed in the polar regions during the summer then migrate to warmer regions to give birth to their young.

The breeding cycle of females was the first seasonal change to be examined. It was found from the dissections made by the *Discovery* zoologists that the ovaries of whales bore scars, called *corpora albicantia*, and that each one represented the liberation of an egg. In most mammals these scars gradually disappear, but they persist in rorquals. By counting the scars on the ovaries of a whale the number of ovulations can be determined, but the great problem was to find out how often a whale ovulated. If once a year, then the age of the whale equalled the number of scars plus the number of years from birth to puberty. As whales were thought to ovulate about once a year, counting scars only gave an approximate age in years but it was useful in assigning a relative age to female whales so that average ages of different populations or variations in average age could be determined.

Ovary scars can, of course, be found only in females but there are two characters common to both sexes of rorquals which continue to grow throughout life. Baleen plates grow continuously from the gum of the upper jaw and each one is inscribed with irregular ridges that represent variations in the rate of growth. Unfortunately, like fingernails, the continuous growth of baleen plates is balanced by the wearing away of the tip so that only a few ridges are present in older whales. However, counting the ridges is a means of ageing young whales and has allowed the age of puberty to be determined.

The best method so far found of calculating the age of a whale was discovered by P. E. Purves while he was studying the mechanism of hearing. Blocking the outer passage of the ear is a long, horny 'plug' which conducts sound to the eardrum (see Chapter 4). When cut down the middle each earplug reveals a series of growth layers where material has been laid down. These layers, or laminae, are found in both sexes and do not get worn away, so they appear to be perfect indicators of age.

The difficulty is, once again, to find the rate at which the laminae are laid down. They could be formed annually or biennially, depending on what physiological changes control the laying down of the horny material. When the laminae were compared with the accumulation of ovary scars, it seemed likely that two laminae are laid down each year but more direct evidence is given by marking live whales. One fin whale was captured by whalers twenty-five years after it had been marked and its earplugs bore twenty-eight laminae. Clearly they could not have accumulated at a rate of two per year but a rate of one per year is possible if marking had taken place at the age of three years. On the other hand, humpbacks marked when very small have been caught five years later with ten or more laminae.

The problem with finding methods of age determination in all animals is how to mark them when very young so that animals of known age can be obtained in later years and the methods of age determination checked accurately. In some groups of animals this has been quite easy. Birds are conveniently marked by placing a numbered ring on the leg; fish are tagged with discs pinned to their bodies; and land mammals have their ears clipped or tagged. None of these methods can be used for whales, nor can branding, which has been used on seals.

The method of marking whales which is now used with considerable success for showing the movements of whales was at first accidental. In the days of hand-harpooning it was not unusual for a whale to get away with one or more harpoons stuck in its back. Years later, perhaps, it would be successfully harpooned and the old harpoon heads, still identifiable, found in its flesh. Scientific marking of whales started in the 1920's when the Discovery

Committee scientists tried firing marks like outsize, barbed drawing pins into the backs of whales. The idea was for the marks to be clearly visible, but they fell out too easily. The next step was to shoot aluminium, and later stainless steel, darts from a special twelve-bore gun. The dart bore a number, the address of the Discovery Committee and the promise of a £1 reward if the mark and details of its discovery were sent in.

The method was a success, so marking became a practical proposition and, between 1926 and 1939, 5,350 whales were marked by *Discovery* expeditions, mainly from the *William Scoresby*, a small ship built on the lines of a whale-catcher. The use of a ship for whale-marking is very expensive but since World War II, some eight nations have marked whales from special ships, whalecatchers or helicopters.

Marking with darts has one great drawback. To lodge securely the dart has to penetrate deep into the muscles of the back. This means that it is unlikely to be discovered until the whale is almost dismembered at the factory, by which time much vital material, such as the earplugs and ovaries, may be lost. Worse still, the dart may be missed completely and only discovered when the meat boilers are cleaned out. By this time it will be impossible to tell from which whale it came. Nevertheless, marking has yielded results. Of the 5,350 whales marked by Discovery Committee ships, nearly 300 were recovered by 1939 although less than 100 more were found during the next twenty years.

The results from marking programmes have not been particularly helpful in the problem of ageing whales, except in a few instances like those mentioned above. This is because it is impossible to find out much about a whale at the time that the dart is inserted. There will be no indication of its age unless it is a calf, but marking a calf has a drawback in that there is the danger of a dart severely wounding it. The programmes have yielded more useful information about the migrations of whales, which shows that whales from one summer feeding ground migrate to a particular breeding area in winter, and that a group from one area often keep separate from other groups.

Unfortunately the recovery of a mark does not tell us where a whale went and what it did between marking and capture. One blue whale was caught 1,900 miles from the place of marking after an interval of fifty-seven days. What is not known is whether it swam in a straight line between the two points, whether it cruised evenly at thirty-three miles per day and fed as it travelled, or whether the 1,900 miles was covered in only a fraction of the fifty-seven days.

After World War II, when whaling was resumed again after an almost complete lapse of several years, several countries joined Norway and Britain in promoting research into whale biology. Both scope and scale of the research have increased in consequence. It is now possible to estimate the total numbers of some whale species, and it is abundantly clear that they have been seriously reduced. It is also possible to estimate the rate at which baby whales are born into a population, and therefore the rate at which a species can be hunted or at which it will recover if hunting is checked, although the precise figures may be disputed by different authorities.

Longevity, numbers and birthrate are the practical problems of whale biology which need to be answered if whales are to survive; but there is also an increasing interest by zoologists in the behaviour of whales: their courtship and family life, and their ability to dive to great depths, locate food and navigate in the vast volume of the sea. The large cetaceans do not lend themselves easily to such studies and the bulk of our knowledge of cetacean behaviour comes from observations on the smaller species which are kept in marine aquaria. For the whales, information has come from the whalers and from observant crewmen of merchant and naval vessels. When gathered together, such accounts give an idea of the habits of the giants of the animal world and to some extent it is allowable to use the studies on captive dolphins to draw conclusions about the behaviour of whales; but it is really necessary to find ways of observing them in the wild at close quarters. This is a more difficult task than formerly because there are fewer whales to watch. However, some advances have been made, as in the pioneer work of Roger Payne, who has followed humpback whales in a small boat to record their incredible songs (see Chapter 6).

3. Life at Sea

Three groups of mammals have taken to the sea: the seals, the sea-cows and the cetaceans. The seals are a marine family of carnivores which, although beautifully adapted for swimming and able to search for food in deep water, betray their terrestrial ancestry by the retention of the hindlimbs, as flippers. The fur seals and sealions can turn their hindlimbs forward and lift the body clear of the ground when bounding along the shore. The true seals, which include the common and grey seals of European coasts, are unable to use their hindlimbs for movement on land. Some species do not even use their front flippers, and have to move by hitching their bodies along. Nevertheless all seals come ashore or on to ice floes to give birth.

The manatees and the dugong of the sea-cow order *Sirenia* are superficially like the whales in appearance. The skin is hairless, the forelimbs are paddle-shaped, the hindlimbs are missing and the tail is expanded horizontally into flukes. Sirenians rarely, if ever, come ashore, and the young are born in the water. Their ribs are weak so that their lungs would be squashed by the weight of the body on land and the skin cracks if it is allowed to dry out. Although the sirenians spend their whole lives in the water, they do not seem to be as fully aquatic as the seals. They stay near the shore in calm water and cannot stay underwater for long.

It is the cetaceans that have completely conquered the sea and have cut free from the land to colonize the oceans. They can be considered a very successful group of animals in both their abundance and diversity, and this may be due to the lack of competition with other mammals once they left the land. A whole new world was opened to them during the course of their evolution which they have exploited in two main ways. One group, the whalebone whales, became specialized for feeding on the swarms of small floating animals. The abundance of this food allowed them to develop body sizes that are impossible to attain on land. The others, the toothed whales, became carnivores, feeding mainly on fish and squid. Except for the sperm whale, the toothed whales do not approach the whalebone whales in size, but they have made up for this in diversity. The small porpoises and dolphins do not concern us here, but they are to be found at sea, inshore and even far up rivers and in lakes.

The first requirement of an aquatic animal is the ability to swim and it is to this end that a whale's body is organized. The body of a whale is very fishlike and its method of swimming also bears a close resemblance to the movements of fishes. The flippers of a whale and the pectoral fins of a fish are used only for steering and balance. The propulsive effort comes from the beating of the tail which is transmitted to the water by the broad surfaces of the flukes or tail fins.

In whales the trunk of the body is very rigid, but the tail is flexible and is

Figure 2 Diagrammatic representation of the swimming movements of a whale, showing the forward-directed forces acting on the flukes.

hinged at its point of attachment to the lumbar region of the back, at the region of the vestigial pelvis. The lumbar region is the powerhouse of the whale and contains massive muscles which are attached by long tendons to the vertebrae in the tail. These muscles contract rhythmically to raise and lower the tail stock, which is flattened from side to side to reduce resistance to its movement through the water. The power generated in the lumbar muscles and tail are released through the flukes, flat blades of tough fibres that pivot at the tip of the tail so that, at every phase of the tail's beat, they are forcing water backwards and the whale forwards (Figure 2). The tail can also swing sideways to alter the direction of the thrust, so that the whale is power-steered like a boat with an outboard motor.

The work of the propulsive unit is made easier by the streamlining of the body, which is shaped like the fuselage of an aeroplane, with a broad nose, tapering towards the rear. Any projections, like ears, are reduced to a minimum, or eliminated. The skin is very smooth and virtually hairless, although whales can be fouled by barnacles and other clinging animals in the same way as the hull of a ship. One humpback whale was found to have 1,000 lbs of barnacles adhering to it and it is said that humpbacks migrating up the west coast of Africa will move towards the coast where the Congo River flows into the sea and the relatively fresh water will kill off their barnacles. It is also said that sailing vessels used to be brought there for the same purpose.

The power produced by the large rorquals is immense. They can leap clear of the water and, when harpooned, have been known to tow catcher boats weighing several hundred tons. The maximum speed that whales can attain is not easy to measure, particularly as there is a great difference between the short burst of a sprinter and the steady pace of a long-distance runner. Under natural conditions whales have little need to move at more than a steady pace, although the toothed whales need to dash after their prey. The right whales are the dawdlers among whales, cruising at 2–5 mph and making 10 mph over short distances when chased. Humpbacks are also slow movers and the sperm whale averages 10 mph with short bursts of up to 20 mph. Rorquals are the fastest, as well as the largest, whales and even modern motor whalecatchers cannot catch up with them without effort. The normal speed of blue and fin whales is about 12 mph and they can sprint up to 20 mph for 10–15 minutes, perhaps to 30 mph or more over very short distances. The fastest whale is the slender sei whale which has been reported as reaching 35 knots for a very short time.

Very occasionally some whales will leap clear of the sea, apparently for fun, but as a general rule they come to the surface only to breathe or 'blow'. The minimum possible time is spent changing the air in the lungs and very little of the body is exposed during the process. As little as two or three seconds are spent in blowing, which is audible as a loud sigh or whistle, but a part of the whale is visible for another four or five seconds as its head goes down and its back rises then slips out of view. Several blows follow in quick succession, after which the whale dives or 'sounds' and is not seen again for a good few minutes. Sperm or humpback whales flip their flukes out of the water before finally disappearing, leaving a slick on the water. Rorquals stay under for 5–10 minutes but the sperm whale usually stays under for twenty minutes. The duration of a sound depends on what the whale is doing; whether it is feeding, cruising slowly or hurrying. When whales are pursued and are fleeing at speed they have to surface to blow more frequently, and after a very prolonged dive a whale has to lie panting at the surface.

Each time a whale blows a characteristic plume of vapour bursts from its blowhole. In mediaeval pictures this was depicted as a fountain of water and whales were said to spout. While the blow is definitely not a jet of water, there is no certainty about how it is formed. It used to be thought that it was a cloud formed by condensation of vapour in the breath, such as we produce on a cold day when our warm breath mingles with cold air, but this cannot be the complete answer as blows can be seen in the warm air of the tropics. A recent explanation is that exhalation blows water and oil from the breathing passages as a fine spray. The ears of whales are surrounded by air sacs which connect with the trachea, or windpipe. The air sacs are filled with an oily foam which is secreted from glands (see p. 44). It is thought that, at each blow, some of this foam is sucked out with the rush of air and hangs in the air as a fine cloud.

It is quite likely that both condensation of water vapour and the oily foam contribute to the whale's blow but, whatever the cause, it is the blow that is the first, and often only, sight that one gets of a whale. Depending on conditions the blow may rise for twenty feet and hang for a few seconds before dispersing. With experience this is sufficient to identify a whale. Right whales can be distinguished by a double, v-shaped blow, rorquals have a single blow, and the blow of sperm whales rises at a steep angle, rather than vertically (Figure 3).

Figure 3 From left to right, the blows of a right whale, a fin whale and a sperm whale.

Little is seen of whales. But they live not far beneath the surface of the sea, at depths where sunlight still penetrates. The small floating animals on which whalebone whales feed are most abundant in the top thirty feet of the sea and it is rare for these whales to go farther down. The toothed whales, and the sperm whale in particular, need to descend to greater depths in search of fish and squid.

The depths reached by sperm whales during their regular dives are not known, but they have sometimes been found entangled in submarine cables. The record is held by the recovery of a sperm whale skeleton from a cable lying on the seabed at 3,700 feet. It is assumed that the whale was feeding when its jaw became entangled in the cable. Other sperm whales have been found at rather lesser depths and a killer whale has been found entangled in a cable at 3,400 feet.

The ability of whales, and other marine animals, to dive to such depths raises several important problems. Even with breathing apparatus a human diver has difficulty descending to depths of a couple of hundred feet, because of the incredible pressure that is exerted by the weight of water as he goes down. For each thirty feet of the descent the pressure increases by one atmosphere (about 15 lbs per square inch) so that a deep-diving sperm whale encounters pressures of a hundred atmospheres, or half a ton per square inch. To prevent the lungs from being flooded by water being forced into the air passages, the blowhole is kept watertight by powerful elastic lips, and in the deep-diving odontocetes there is a system of blocks and valves formed by the air sacs around the nasal passage.

Figure 4 Diagrams of a sperm whale head in (a) side view and (b) top view to show the breathing passages (after Raven and Gregory). Note the single blowhole which is off-centre.

There would also be a danger of water being forced down the windpipe as the odontocete whale feeds if its windpipe connected to the throat in the same way as in man. We can breathe through the mouth as well as through the nostrils, the two airstreams meeting at the top of the throat to pass into the windpipe. In whales the epiglottis at the top of the windpipe is extended in the form of a 'beak' to fit into the nasal passage, so separating the feeding and breathing routes. This is however not essential, as whalebone whales and other mammals, including man, can eat and swallow under water with safety. It could be that the 'beak' is important for the toothed whales which feed at great depths where the pressure is very great, and that it also prevents air from escaping through the mouth when water pressure is squeezing the lungs.

One of the great dangers to human divers is decompression sickness, or the 'bends', caused by breathing air supplied at the same high pressure as the surrounding water so that a large amount of nitrogen from the air accumulates in solution in their bodies. Nitrogen is the main constituent of air and it is not poisonous under normal circumstances but, because it is not involved in any of the body's metabolic processes, it remains in the bloodstream and tissues. It does no harm there, but a diver breathing under pressure accumulates a large amount of nitrogen in his tissues, and when he surfaces the pressure is released and the nitrogen bubbles out of solution, like the bubbles of carbon dioxide rising from a bottle of tonic water when the cap is removed. Any bubbles of oxygen are soon used up by the body but bubbles of nitrogen persist and are extremely damaging. They collect in the blood vessels where they form painful and sometimes fatal airlocks and, because nitrogen is absorbed particularly by fatty tissues, bubbles are especially liable to appear in the fatty coverings of nerve fibres, where they disrupt the functioning of the nerves and cause paralysis.

The 'bends' are prevented by the diver surfacing slowly so that the pressure is gently relaxed and the nitrogen has time to dissolve out of the blood and be passed out through the lungs. An alternative is for the diver to breathe a gas mixture that does not contain nitrogen. The whales' solution to this problem is simple. They are not exposed to the risk of bends in the first place because they submerge with only the nitrogen contained in one deep breath and this becomes dissolved in the body fluids only at atmospheric pressure. Furthermore, nitrogen in the air passages and lungs is believed to be absorbed by the oily foam in the breathing passages.

To be able to survive a long dive (a maximum of over one hour for sperm whales) with only the air contained in the lungs a careful husbanding of oxygen supplies is essential. A whale's lungs are surprisingly small for the size of its body and they carry only about one tenth of the oxygen stored for use in a dive. A pearl-diver working without diving apparatus, on the other hand, carries a third of his oxygen store in the lungs. In whales a large amount of oxygen is stored in the muscles where it is bound to myoglobin, a substance related to oxygen-carrying haemoglobin in the blood. Like haemoglobin, myoglobin is dark red and the large quantities found in the muscles of diving animals accounts for their almost black meat. The precious store of oxygen is conserved by the almost complete shut-down of inessential body activities. The heartbeat slows down (from 110 to 50 beats per minute in the bottlenose dolphin) and the blood circulation shuts down, except to supply the vital functions of the heart and nervous system.

During the dive the swimming muscles, which must, of course, keep going, function without oxygen. They get their energy from anaerobic respiration. This is the process by which carbohydrates are partially oxidized to form lactic acid and release energy without the use of oxygen. The lactic acid is stored until the whale surfaces. It then pants, or 'has its spoutings out' as the whalers termed it, inhaling oxygen to break down the lactic acid and exhaling the carbon dioxide formed in the process. This is the same mechanism as is used by a human sprinter. During a short burst of speed the lungs cannot supply sufficient oxygen; an 'oxygen debt' is built up and has to be repaid by panting afterwards.

It must be realized that the information a dead whale can supply is limited and much of our knowledge of the mechanisms in living whales is speculative. It has been possible to measure the heartbeat of captive dolphins in marine aquaria, but it can only be surmised that the same thing happens when a blue whale dives. There is much of the physiology of whales that is a mystery, or at least open to debate. The function of the enormous bulbous forehead of the sperm whale with its case of spermaceti has been the subject of several theories. The most recent suggestion has come from Malcolm Clarke, of the National Institute of Oceanography, who considers it possible that the case is acting as a buoyancy tank.

The density of seawater increases with depth and, therefore, a whale will become more buoyant as it dives. To counteract this buoyancy, Clarke suggests, the spermaceti, which is liquid at blood heat, is cooled by the surrounding seawater and sets as a wax, thus contracting and becoming more dense. The change in density of the spermaceti has been calculated by Clarke to be sufficient to overcome the increased buoyancy due to the increase in density of the seawater. The density of the spermaceti can be controlled by djusting its temperature, through regulating the rate of flow of blood in the case. Thus the whale stays neutrally buoyant at any depth and it does not have to waste energy in maintaining its depth. When it needs to surface it can come up like a submarine without physical effort, by pumping blood through the capillaries in the case. The spermaceti warms up, becoming less dense and lifting the whale to the surface.

4. Submarine Senses

Like any other animal, a whale needs to be aware of its surroundings; to know the physical conditions of temperature, light and gravity; to know where its fellows are and to obtain its food. It is able to do this through its sense organs, each of which collects specific information to enable the animal to conduct its activities properly. Man relies principally on sight, with hearing playing an important part and smell, touch and taste filling minor roles. These are the traditional five senses and the relative importance of each is different in various animals. Dogs, for instance, place a great reliance on smell; while bats make use of an acute sense of hearing for their echo-location and can hear high pitched sounds far beyond the range of our ears.

It is not surprising, therefore, to find that the whales are equipped with senses that differ considerably from ours. Their sense organs have to function underwater and this immediately imposes restrictions on mechanisms which were evolved by terrestrial ancestors living in air. Vision is our main sense but as soon as we dive underwater it becomes obvious that eyesight is of limited use. Even in the clearest water it is impossible to make out objects at a distance greater than about fifty feet. The turbidity of seawater results in a much lower visibility in practice, and visibility wanes rapidly with increasing depth. At thirty feet only one tenth of the sunlight remains and at 1,300 feet it is pitch dark. Consequently vision can only be of limited use, even to whalebone whales feeding near the surface. It is useless for sperm whales diving deep for squid.

There is a second drawback to vision underwater for an animal with eyes designed for use in air. When we swim underwater without the benefit of a face mask our eyes become longsighted (Figure 5). The image on the retina is formed by the refraction of light as it passes through the eye. In air, the curvature of the lens accounts for only a small part of the total refraction, the major part of the focusing of light on to the retina is due to refraction at the surface of the cornea. This depends on the difference between the refractive index of the corneal tissue and that of air and on the curvature of the cornea. In other words, the cornea is acting as an extra lens. When underwater, the eye loses the benefit of corneal refraction because the refractive indices of water and corneal tissue are almost identical and the light is not bent

Figure 5 Vision in whales and man. In air a whale's eye becomes shortsighted because light is focused in front of the retina; in water a man becomes longsighted because light is focused behind the retina.

as it passes from one to the other. The only refraction remaining is that at the lens and the result is longsightedness. The image is formed behind the retina and objects appear blurred.

To compensate for this deficiency, the eye of a whale has an almost spherical lens, for the more curved a lens the greater is its focusing power. Spherical lenses are also found in the eyes of seals and fishes, showing this to be a common solution to the problem. There are other adaptations for a marine environment. Tear glands are unnecessary as the eye is continually bathed in salt water but to protect them against the wear of the water streaming past, an oily substance is secreted from the corners of the eyes and the surface of the cornea is unusually tough. The sclera, or outside coat, of the eyeball is also very thick and tough, and this prevents the eyeball being distorted by water pressure when the whale dives.

In general, then, it appears that whales have passably good eyes, and, to compensate for the dim light, there is the tapetum, a layer of reflective material, lying behind the retina. It is the tapetum that causes a cat's eyes to shine in the dark, its function being to reflect light back to the retina a second time so that the sensitivity of vision is increased. Nevertheless, vision must still play a relatively minor role in the lives of whales because of the position of the eyes on the head. It is clearly impossible for the large whalebone whales to see anything that is not to the side and the poor visibility will prevent them from seeing farther than one body's length away.

Among the toothed whales, the sperm whales are at a similar disadvantage, even when they hunt in shallow water where there is appreciable light. The whalers used to approach sperm whales from the front or rear where the whales could not see them. There is a record of a pilot whale that ignored food placed in front of its snout because it could not see it there, but bottle-nosed dolphins have their eyes set far enough forward for stereoscopic vision and the excellence of their vision is shown by the feats of captive dolphins leaping clear of their pools to take titbits from the trainer's hand.

If the great drawback to vision underwater is that light does not penetrate far, sound, on the other hand, travels very well through water so it is not surprising to find that hearing is the whale's most important sense. A human diver cannot hear well and completely loses the ability to locate the source of a sound, because, as with the eyes, his ears are designed for use in air. The whales have evolved modifications that enable their ears to work efficiently underwater. These changes become clear in a comparison of the structure of a whale's ear with that of a land mammal.

The ear of mammals is divided into outer, middle and inner parts. The outer ear consists of a tube, the meatus, leading into the head and ending at a membrane, the eardrum, which separates it from the middle ear. Around the opening of the meatus is a flap of cartilage, the pinna, which collects sound waves and directs them into the meatus. The waves travel down the meatus and strike the eardrum, setting up vibrations which are carried through three small bones, the auditory ossicles. The ossicles lie in the air-filled cavity of the middle ear and hinge together like a series of levers, amplifying the vibrations and transmitting them to the fluid-filled tubes of the inner ear.

The inner ear consists of the semicircular canals, the organ of balance and not concerned with hearing, and the cochlea, a spiral tube equipped with a set of sense cells that register vibrations in the surrounding fluid and transmit the information to the brain.

To summarise, the mammalian ear collects vibrations from the air, amplifies and converts them into vibrations in the fluid of the inner ear so that the sense cells can be stimulated. The mechanism of the whale ear follows the same basic pattern but it is adapted to collect vibrations from water (Figure 6). It also has to function efficiently under great pressures.

Figure 6 A diagrammatic section through the ear of a whale.

The whale has no earflap or pinna, which would be an obstruction to streamlining; all that can be seen of the ear is a small slit in the skin which leads to a very narrow meatus. In fin whales and other whalebone whales it is just possible to push a little finger into the meatus but the central part of the meatus closes completely and is no more than a string of connective tissue. It then opens out again into a narrow tube which runs to the eardrum. This is a more complex structure than the simple drum-like membrane of the human ear. In whalebone whales the membrane of the eardrum is in the form of a taut ligament attached to a ring of bone and an elongated tube like the finger of a glove which lies in the meatus. Fitting over the 'glove finger' and blocking up the meatus is the 'ear-plug' of concentric layers of horny material which is used in determining the age of whalebone whales (see Chaper 3).

Vibrations in the surrounding water are transmitted down the meatus, the parallel fibres of the connective tissues making up the closed section being a better conductor of sound than the surrounding blubber. The earplug is also a good sound conductor and it carries sounds to the eardrum and sets the three auditory ossicles in motion. From there onwards, there is little difference between the working of the ears of land mammals and whales, except that the ossicles of the whale's ear are arranged to give a greater amplification and provision has to be made for the ear to work under pressure.

For the eardrum and ossicles to vibrate freely it is necessary for the air pressure in the middle ear to have a presure equal to that of the medium on the outside of the eardrum. In land mammals this is maintained by the eustachian tube, a narrow tube running from the middle ear to the throat. Changes of pressure on the outside of the eardrum are balanced by a valve in the eustachian tube allowing air in or out of the middle ear. An increase in external pressure caused by diving or even driving down a steep hill forces the eardrums in and gives rise to a feeling of discomfort in the ears. We relieve this by 'swallowing' and allowing air to pass up the eustachian tube so that pressures on each side of the eardrums are equalized and the ossicles are allowed to vibrate freely.

A whale cannot swallow in this manner and its eustachian tubes end in large air sacs surrounding the ears. As the whale dives and the pressure around it increases, the air sacs are squeezed and air is forced into the middle ear to counteract the increased pressure on the outside of the eardrum. The constrictive effect of pressure is also counteracted by two muscles attached to the ligament of the eardrum. These contract to equalize the inward movement of the eardrum and allow the ossicles to move freely.

So far it has been explained how the whale ear is adapted to convert sound in water to vibrations of the ossicles in the middle ear and how it can do this despite wide variations in pressure; but the whale still faces the problems that make the human ear inefficient underwater. In a land animal sound waves travel through the air-filled passage of the outer ear and therefore have to pass along the ossicles where they are amplified. The sound waves cannot pass directly from the air to the bone of the skull and so cannot bypass the eardrum and auditory ossicles and stimulate the sense cells in the cochlea directly. When underwater, the eardrum and ossicles can be bypassed because sound passes easily from water through bone and directly to the cochlea. The amplifying effect of the ossicles is consequently lost and hearing is impaired.

Conduction of sound through the skull also prevents a human diver from telling the position of a source of sound. The direction of a sound is judged by the minute difference in time that it reaches each ear, or by a minute difference in the loudness in each ear. If a sound comes from a source directly in front of the head, it will reach both ears simultaneously but if the source is moved to the left, the sound will reach the left ear first. The head also acts as a barrier so that sound waves have to travel round it to enter the right ear. When underwater the head ceases to be a barrier and sound waves travel direct to both ears.

Whales have overcome the difficulty of the conduction of sound from water to bone by a number of devices that isolate the ear mechanism from the skull so that it responds only to sounds passing down the meatus and through the ossicles. The bones that surround the ear are very dense and so hard that it is very difficult to saw them without their splintering. The high density prevents them from resonating when the lighter bones of the skull vibrate. Furthermore, these bones are not intimately attached to the skull, as in other mammals, but are loosely attached by connective tissue which does not conduct sound well. The ear bones of whales can be wrenched off the skull by hand and they are sometimes found washed up on beaches. The space between these ear bones and the skull is filled by the air sacs leading from the eustachian tube (see Chapter 2). They are filled with an oily foam secreted by glands in their walls which forms another barrier to sound coming through the skull.

It was only in 1954 that F. C. Fraser and P. E. Purves of the British Museum (Natural History) demonstrated these mechanisms, and showed that whales hear in exactly the same manner as other mammals but with special adaptations to make this possible. Until this time no one had been able to see how whales had overcome the problem of conduction of sound through bone. The first scientists to write on the subject considered that whales had a poor sense of hearing, but their speculations were not based on observations of the behaviour of live animals.

It had in fact been known from ancient times that whales and their relatives have good hearing. Pliny recorded that bottlenosed dolphins along the coast of the Black Sea were attracted with special whistles, and the traditional method of porpoise hunting in the Solomon Islands is to drive the porpoises ashore, scaring them by clashing stones together underwater (see Chapter 8). The whalers of the eighteenth and nineteenth centuries knew that they had to approach sperm whales very cautiously as the splash of an oar or the thump of a foot against a plank alerted the whales and sent them fleeing.

Recent experiments on the hearing of dolphins have shown that they have a sense of hearing second only to that of bats. Bottlenosed dolphins can hear sounds up to a pitch of 153 kilocycles, compared with an upper limit of 175 kilocycles for the hearing of bats and a mere 20 kilocycles for man. The upper limit of hearing for whales is not known and, in any case, it is most likely that, as with bats and porpoises, they are most sensitive to sounds within a range somewhat below the upper limit. It is known, however, that whalebone whales are sensitive to asdic which transmits tones of 20 to 40 kilocycles. This sensitivity has limited the use of asdic for whale hunting along the lines of submarine hunting, but it has been used in the method of whaling called *prøyser jag* in which whales are chased and so forced to surface at short intervals to breathe (see Chapter 12). It is also known that the ears of whales show anatomical features connected with a sensitivity to high tones. The earplug is a particularly good conductor of high tones and one of the ossicles is attached to the middle ear by bony rather than by soft tissue, a condition also found in bats. There is also evidence that the cochlea is particularly sensitive to high tones.

The sensitivity of the whale ear can be demonstrated by anatomical investigation and simple observations such as those described above, but it is a much harder task to find out what whales are using their ears for. By analogy with land mammals, it would seem that whales could use their ears for listening for prey and enemies or for communicating with their fellows. A further possibility is that, as their hearing is extremely sensitive, they may, like bats, use a system of echo-location or sonar to find their prey or to detect obstacles in the water.

It is the use of sonar by cetaceans that has received the greatest interest since it has been found that dolphins kept in captivity can avoid swimming into nets even when the water is very murky. The ease of training dolphins to carry out tests under controlled conditions has led to the discovery that they have an extremely sensitive form of sonar. For instance, one dolphin was trained to swim towards the larger of a pair of metal balls suspended in the water while wearing rubber cups over the eyes. It was frequently able to distinguish a $2\frac{1}{2}$ inch sphere from a $2\frac{1}{4}$ inch sphere. Other experiments have shown that dolphins can distinguish the texture of different objects, and even discriminate between kinds of fish they like and dislike by means of sonar.

Dolphins locate and identify objects by emitting a stream of extremely powerful, very short clicks. They would be deafening to us except that they are of extremely short duration and, although audible, most of their energy is emitted at very high frequencies (up to 100 kilocycles) and well beyond the range of our hearing. The clicks probably originate in the region of the glottis, in the windpipe, and are focused into a narrow beam of sound by the oily 'melon' in the forehead. Echoes are reflected from objects in front of the dolphin and picked up and identified. Most surprisingly, there is evidence that the echoes are not received through the outer and middle ears, but are transmitted up the hollow, oil-filled bones of the lower jaw to the dense bones surrounding the ears.

The existence of sonar has been proved only in the dolphins kept in marine aquaria, but streams of clicks, of the same sort as those emitted by echo-locating dolphins, have been recorded from sperm whales. There is no reason to suppose that sperm whales do not use sonar, and it is difficult to think how else they can capture squid in the pitch darkness of the depths. There is less evidence for the ability of whalebone whales to use sonar, as there has been little success in recording any sounds from them that can be interpreted as part of an echo-locating mechanism. Yet, as with the sperm whale, they must have some method of locating their food and their ears are sufficiently well developed for the possession of an echo-locating ability to be feasible.

The use of the voice for communication between whales has only recently received serious study. The voices of whales have been known as long as their sense of hearing. The ancient Greeks knew that dolphins sometimes uttered groans and squeals and British whalers of the eighteenth century gave the beluga the name 'sea canary' because they could sometimes hear it trilling like a songbird. Observations in marine aquaria show that the trills are accompanied by a stream of bubbles from the blowhole, and as whales lack vocal chords, the sounds are probably generated by air flowing past folds in the larynx.

The function of the various calls that have been recorded is most likely to keep a group of animals in contact with each other. Such calls are found in other mammals that live in groups and they inform each individual of the whereabouts of its companions and enable it to avoid becoming separated. That this is a likely explanation for the calls of whales is being revealed by the exciting discoveries of Roger Payne whose work on the 'songs' of humpback whales is described in Chapter 6.

Our studies on the hearing of whales and the ways in which they make use of this sense are far from complete, yet it is quite clear that hearing is the principal sense by which a whale gathers information about its environment. Sight plays no more than a secondary role and the other senses have little or no importance.

The sense of smell can play little part in the life of an animal that spends most of its life underwater with its nostrils shut. Clearly a whale would choke if it allowed water to pass down its nasal passages so there is no way of getting odiferous molecules to the organ of smell. Indeed, toothed whales have no organ of smell and no olfactory bulb, the part of the brain concerned with smelling. Whalebone whales do have a simple organ of smell, an olfactory nerve and a small olfactory bulb. Presumably they can detect smells when they blow, but what use this is to them is not known. Taste is also very rudimentary in whales, although this is the sensation of chemicals dissolved in water and so might be considered important in a marine animal. However, it is a general rule that a poor sense of taste is found in animals which swallow their food whole, as do whales. The toothed whales seem to have a slight sense of taste, but even this appears to be lacking in whalebone whales.

Compared with smell and taste, the sense of touch is well developed. Dolphins kept in marine aquaria are very sensitive to touch. They are fond of being stroked and patted, and will rub their bodies against objects. This shows a general sensitivity to touch on the body but there are also pits on the snout which are the remains of hair follicles in the new-born calf. Each pit is richly supplied by nerves and may be sensitive to changes in water pressure. There are similar organs of touch around the lips of whalebone whales, which are known to be very sensitive. They have been examined in sei whales, and presumably they will be found in other rorquals.

A sei whale has about eighty short, stiff hairs, between half an inch and an inch long, disposed about its upper and lower lips. Each one has what appear to be touch sense cells grouped around the root and it has been suggested that they are used for sensing the flow of water past the body or low frequency vibrations. Sensation of water flow would give the hairs the function of a speedometer, and the ability to detect low frequencies might be helpful in navigation as they would be set up by the movements of prey and the swirling of water around rocks and other objects. Other supposed organs of touch are small tubercles, about one millimetre across, which are found inside the lips, around the lining of the mouth and on the tongue. These may also be for sensing food and water movements, but like so much else about the senses of these large and inaccessible animals we have no means of telling.

1. The replica of an eighty-foot blue whale. It is a cast from a carcase of a whale caught off Norway

3. The fibrous ends of whalebone form a sieve on each side of the long.

2. Section of the earplug of a baleen whale, showing the growth lines

5. Sieving Shrimps and Catching Squid

Since the days of Jonah there have been misconceptions as to the size and sort of food eaten by whales. The story of Jonah is an allegory, but there are many stories of whales attacking and devouring men among the legends of seagoing peoples. Despite such stories there are no proven records of man-eating or even of deliberate mankilling by whales, although many whales lash out at or charge their pursuers. Even the killer whale, the only cetacean to prey on large vertebrates, has never been proved guilty of homicide.

It has long been realized that the whalebone whales were unable to swallow large prey. John Evelyn, the diarist, told of a whale, evidently a right whale, that was stranded in the Thames below London in 1658. He described the throat as being so small that not even the smallest fish could pass through it, but Evelyn had not realized that the throat collapses after death. Nearer the present day, Rudyard Kipling was also unaware of this when he wrote the story of 'How the Whale Got his Throat'. The whale in his *Just-So* story started as a maneater and swallowed a shipwrecked mariner on his raft. Eventually the mariner was put ashore, like Jonah, but before leaving the whale he blocked its throat with a grating made from his raft, and ever afterwards the whale could eat nothing 'except very, very small fish'. To anyone raised on Kipling's *Just-So Stories* it may come as a surprise that whalebone whales can feed on fish and sometimes swallow seabirds as large as penguins and cormorants. Their main food is, however, small floating animals, particularly the shrimp-like animals known as krill. Collectively, these animals are called plankton, a Greek word meaning 'that which drifts'. Plankton includes minute floating plants and animals that do no more than float passively in the water and small animals such as crustaceans, jellyfish, sea snails, sea urchin larvae and many others that have limited powers of movement but in general are just swept around by the currents.

Anyone looking over the side of a boat into clear seawater will be lucky to see anything drifting or swimming in it but closer examination may reveal myriads of small, almost transparent, animals. These are of more than passing interest because they are the key to life in the sea and are the means by which the whales, millions of times larger, are sustained. The basis of this floating life are minute plants, called phytoplankton. Like the familiar plants on land, they make their food by photosynthesis, absorbing sunlight and using its energy to build carbon dioxide and water into carbohydrates. The plants of the phytoplankton breed prolifically and are eaten in colossal numbers by the small animals, the zooplankton. They, in turn, form the food of the familiar animals: fish, squid, seabirds and the whalebone whales.

The succession of eaters and eaten is known as a food chain, and the food chain of the whalebone whales is one of the simplest that exists. It is: phytoplankton→zooplankton→whales (see Figure 7), although it is now known

Figure 7 Food chains of whales.

that many whales also feed on fish which, themselves, feed on zooplankton.

The food chain of whalebone whales has been especially studied in the Antarctic, first by the scientists of the British *Discovery* expeditions and later by those of other nations. It might be thought that the cold waters of the Antarctic would have little life but it turned out that they are amongst the richest in the world. In the Southern Ocean water rich in nutrient salts wells up to the surface to feed the phytoplankton and the organisms sink slowly so they spend more time in the surface zone where photosynthesis can take place.

Chief among the small animals feeding on the masses of Antarctic phytoplankton are animals about $2\frac{1}{2}$ inches long that resemble, but are not related to, shrimps. Their scientific name is *Euphausia* but they are commonly known as krill (Figure 9, p. 54). Krill are found near the surface of the sea because the phytoplankton on which they feed must live at the surface where plenty of sunlight penetrates. In places they gather in vast swarms visible to the naked eye as red-brown patches, up to a quarter of a mile long and two hundred yards across. These huge concentrations are probably brought together by eddy currents and they may persist for several weeks. They are densest in the centre where there may be about 1 lb of krill per cubic foot of water.

The average density of krill in Antarctic waters is much less than this, but an indication of the vast amounts present can be given by estimates that have been made of the weight of krill eaten by whales. It is thought that in one day a blue whale eats about four tons, which is about eight million krill, and a fin whale eats just under three tons. Before the whalers reduced their numbers, the total population of whales consumed an estimated 150 million tons of krill during each summer stay in the Antarctic. Now that the stocks of whales have been greatly reduced, with the blue whales and humpbacks almost wiped out, there must be a vast uneaten surplus of krill which could amount to something like 100–150 million tons.

What is happening to this supposed surplus? The Southern Ocean is so vast and remote that it is impossible to attempt accurate estimates of the total krill population and so find out whether their numbers are increasing. It has sometimes been suggested that the other krill-eaters, such as the seabirds, penguins and seals, would increase as the whales diminished. But we have little idea of the total populations of these animals and there is no telling whether the few recorded increases among colonies of Antarctic animals may not be due to changes in climate or other factors unrelated to food supply.

If there is such a vast crop of krill left unharvested now that the whales have gone, the question naturally arises as to whether we could harvest krill for our own use. It takes ten tons of krill to grow one ton of whale, so it would be better to find a way of catching krill and turning it directly into food for human consumption. For many reasons this is not practical at the present. It is better to hunt animals that feed on krill, and now that whales are becoming rare we may find that the best way of exploiting the undoubted riches of the Southern Ocean is to catch Antarctic fish and perhaps crop the seals.

This appears to be a digression from the feeding habits of whalebone whales, but an appreciation of the vast swarms of planktonic animals in the sea makes it easier to understand the feeding mechanism of these whales. Whalebone whales have to subsist on a food that is very abundant. They are huge animals, the largest weighing well over one hundred tons, and, as we have seen, they need several tons of food each day. Therefore their food must be available in enormous quantities. A stickleback can survive by snapping at individual water fleas but a whale cannot afford to select each item of food and must be able to engulf masses of krill with the minimum expenditure of energy.

The fringe of baleen suspended from the upper jaws of whalebone whales is admirably suited to the task, whereas teeth would be virtually useless. The plates act as sieves, removing the krill from the water as it flows between them. Similar mechanisms are found in other animals that feed on plankton. The largest sharks, the whale shark and the basking shark, feed on small crustaceans by straining them on projections of the gills called gill rakers. Herring also possess gill rakers and flamingoes have rows of plates in their bills for sieving out algae. The krill themselves are filter feeders, trapping minute plants and animals on feathery growths at the base of their legs.

The baleen plates are made from the same substance, keratin, as hair and nails. They grow from the gum of the upper jaw and, like nails, are continuously being worn away and replaced. There are 150–400 plates on each side of the mouth, depending on the species of whale. Each plate is less than one-fifth of an inch thick but may be ten or more feet long in right whales. It is made up of hollow fibres enclosed in a horny sheath which gives maximum strength with minimum weight. The plates are set about half an inch apart, and the fibres on the inside edge separate to make a coarse fringe that intermeshes with the fibres of neighbouring plates. This mesh is the strainer which is used for sifting krill from the sea.

No one has ever seen how a whalebone whale feeds but from the structure of the mouth (Figure 8) we can infer what happens. In a right whale the mouth is an enormous vault supported by the huge arches of the upper jaws. From these hang the baleen plates, eight feet long in Biscayan right whales and ten feet in Greenland right whales. These are protected by five-foot high lips rising from the lower jaws. When feeding, a right whale ploughs through the upper layers of the sea with its mouth open. Water gushes in and flows out between the baleen plates where the krill is trapped on the fringe of fibres.

Figure 8 Sections through the head of (a) a right whale and (b) a rorqual, to show the baleen.

At intervals the mouth shuts and the tongue is somehow used to scrape the accumulated krill off the network of fringes and push them back into the throat.

The rorqual whales feed intermittently rather than continuously. Their mouths are not so large as those of right whales (Figure 8) but the folds or pleats that run longitudinally under the head allow the floor of the mouth to drop and increase the volume of the mouth. Rorquals, then, take a series of massive gulps, sucking in large quantities of water, closing the mouth and squeezing the water out through the baleen with the tongue.

A mistaken impression has been given so far that whalebone whales feed solely on krill and that the crustacean *Euphausia* is the only kind of krill. In the Antarctic *Euphausia* is by far the main constituent of krill and the immense studies on Antarctic whales have obscured the fact that, in the Pacific and Atlantic, the krill is made up of close relatives of *Euphausia*, such as *Thysanoessa* and *Meganyctiphanes*, or other small crustaceans such as copepods and amphipods. In sub-Antarctic seas whales feed on 'lobster krill', a crustacean called *Munida*. Whalebone whales also feed on other kinds of animals, such as sea-butterflies or pteropods, known to whalers as 'brit'. These are molluscs, related to winkles and snails, that float in the sea and propel themselves with diaphanous 'wings'. The main food of the Greenland right whale in the Arctic is *Clione* (Figure 9), a sea-butterfly that feeds on other small animals.

Figure 9 Whale food: krill (*Euphausia*) and sea-butterfly (*Clione*).

It is now being found that whalebone whales often feed on much larger prey than planktonic animals and can catch such active animals as herring and squid in sufficient numbers to show that they are not just being swallowed accidentally, like the penguins and cormorants that have occasionally turned up in whale stomachs.

Our knowledge of the diet of whales has come from examination of their stomachs as they are cut up at the factory. This is not so easy a task as it might seem because a whale often vomits when wounded by a harpoon and, even if killed outright, its digestive processes still continue after death. Unless the whale is brought to the factory and immediately cut up, only a thick soup of partly digested animals will be found in its stomach.

Investigations by the *Discovery* scientists showed that the Antarctic whales were feeding almost exclusively on *Euphausia* krill but since World War II the diet of whales has been examined in other parts of the world. Whalebone whales turn out to be much less particular feeders than is generally believed. It is, however, difficult to summarize the diet of any whalebone whale because this varies from place to place. For instance, in the North Pacific minke whales eat fish but these are rarely caught by the Antarctic population.

	Krill	Squid	Sardine	Octopus
Blue whale	50	1	1	0
Fin whale	410	2	1	0
Sei whale	367	145	168	2
Humpback	6	0	1	0
Sperm whale	2	1,513	4	19

Table II. Food caught by whales in Japanese waters (adapted from Mizue). The figures show the number of stomachs containing a particular item.

Table II shows the diets of whales caught in Japanese waters. The surprising figures are those for the sei whale which was once thought to live solely on small plankton as its network of baleen fibres is very fine and woolly. Yet in Japan it has long been known as the 'sardine-whale'. As a general rule it appears that whales with long baleen plates, like the right whales, skim the water for small animals while those with shorter baleen and coarser fringes feed by gulping larger plankton or shoaling fish that can be found in dense masses. Bryde's whale has short plates with coarse, wide-meshed fringes and lives mainly on fish, such as sardines and anchovies, which it finds in tropical seas. Blue, fin and humpback whales have two or three foot-long baleen and are 'gulpers', feeding on whatever is abundant. For the Antarctic blue whale this is almost entirely *Euphausia* but humpbacks and fin whales often feed on fish, the fin whales of the North Atlantic being called 'herring-whales' by the Norwegians and 'herring hogs' by British fishermen.

The sei whale is both a skimmer and a gulper. It has been seen swimming at the surface, skimming up plankton with its fine baleen fringes in the manner of a right whale. But in the Antarctic the sei whale keeps farther north than the other whales, where krill is less abundant. Here it feeds by gulping larger animals, but there is now evidence that since the blue, humpback and fin whales have been killed off, the sei whale has been moving south to feed on krill.

The gray whale is another unusual feeder. It is very rare for any food to be found in its stomach, but the old whalers used to call it the 'mussel-digger' because its snout was often covered in mud. Such food that has been found consists of amphipods which appear to be caught by sieving mud through the coarse, widely-spaced fringes of its baleen.

One of the problems of fishing for krill is how to locate the dense swarms. This has proved difficult for man with his sophisticated instruments, but it is obvious that the whales must be able to do it. It is known that dolphins have a system of echo-location, described in the previous chapter, and we may find that whalebone whales have a similar system, as marine animals from penguins to sealions have now been found to hunt by echo-location. There is also a possibility that the sinus hairs that have been found on the jaws of whalebone whales are somehow used in feeding.

The other great group of whales have entirely different feeding habits, as is suggested by the name alone. Toothed whales feed on large, active prey that must be hunted, caught and swallowed one by one. Most toothed whales are provided with rows of conical, often sharp, teeth and these seem to be the perfect equipment for catching the slippery fish and squid that make up their diets. Yet some toothed whales have virtually no teeth. In most species of beaked whale there are just one or two teeth in the lower jaw and these only appear in later life, if they appear at all. In a few species the teeth never

Figure 10 Jaw bones of (a) a sperm whale and (b) a beaked whale (not to scale).

appear, and only in the Tasmanian beaked whale do all the teeth erupt through the gums. Even the sperm whale, which can have formidable teeth in the lower jaw as well as vestigial ones in the upper jaw, may show no signs of teeth until it is sexually mature.

The absence of well-formed teeth in toothed whales suggests that they need not be used to grasp prey and this is further shown by the finding of barnacles on sperm whale teeth, which indicates a lack of use. It seems that teeth are 'luxuries' and that tough jaws are sufficient to catch fish and squid and toss them back into the throat, unchewed but with the life squeezed out of them. That this is a perfectly sound method of feeding is shown by the many fish-eating birds that seize fish in their horny bills and toss them back.

As hunters of squid and fish, toothed whales need to penetrate to greater depths than the whalebone whales. The sperm whale, in particular, often hunts at great depths where it attacks species of squid hardly known to science. The examination of sperm whale stomachs for the indigestible beaks of squid is one of the best sources of information on this group of animals. It has long been known that sperm whales must fight some of the largest squids, such as *Architeuthis*, a monster growing up to fifty-five feet long, mostly tentacles, and a forty-seven-foot sperm whale harpooned off the Azores was found to have a 405 lb, thirty-four-foot squid in its stomach. Marks made by the suckers of these squids have left scars four inches across on the skin of sperm whales and in 1966 a sperm whale was seen fighting on the surface with *Architeuthis dux*, the largest known squid. Presumably this fight, witnessed off Newfoundland, had started somewhere in the depths and was continued on the surface when the whale ran out of breath. From the remains found in stomachs it is clear that the whale sometimes wins these battles, but we do not know whether the squid sometimes kills the whale or if the fight ever ends in a draw.

Meals of *Architeuthis dux* and its giant relatives must be exceptional, for stomach contents show that sperm whales usually feed on squid only a few feet long. They also feed on fish and octopus (see Table II) and most toothed whales have a varied diet. Some beaked whales are known to eat only cuttle fish but others eat cod, herring and salmon, as well as more unlikely animals such as sea-cucumbers and starfish. The beluga or white whale also feeds on crabs and shrimps, as well as cuttlefish and fish, and sperm whales have sometimes been found with the remains of large sharks and seals in their stomachs.

The killer whale deserves a full discussion as it has the widest diet among the cetaceans, and has been made famous through its cruel treatment of fellow whales. This has, however, led to tales of its ferocity being greatly exaggerated. Firstly, there used to be a notion that the killer whale uses its tall fin to slice open bodies of other whales. This is pure myth. But another widely credited story is due to a misinterpretation of the findings of the nineteenth century biologist Eschricht. He published an account of a stranded killer whale. It measured sixteen feet and he found within it the remains of thirteen porpoises and fourteen seals. This has been taken as twenty-seven whole animals, an impossible figure. What Eschricht really found were fragments of bodies, which must have been accumulated over a fair length of time and were possibly shared with other killers, as they are known to hunt in packs.

The effect of killer whales on other mammals must not be underestimated. The appearance of killers spreads panic amongst seals or sealions, which make for the shore as fast as possible. It is reported that gray whales become so terrified that they can only lie helplessly on their backs and are unable to escape, for killer whales even attack whalebone whales, blue whales included. This is where the charge of cruelty can be upheld, if it is possible to speak of any animal other than man being cruel. Bands of killer whales have been seen attacking large whales, but there is little evidence that they ever kill anything larger than a narwhal or the calf of a whalebone whale; the adults manage to escape with bad cuts. Killer whales do, however, feed on the carcases of large whales and are considered a pest by whalers.

Surprisingly, there is not a single record of maneating by killer whales. The nearest is Herbert Ponting's story of killer whales trying to tip him into the sea. Ponting was the photographer on Captain Scott's expedition to the South Pole and he had gone to the edge of a large ice floe to photograph a school of killer whales. They disappeared underwater then suddenly the floe started to lurch under him. The killer whales were banging it with their backs, causing the ice to split. As Ponting hopped across the ice fragments to safety, large heads heavily armed with teeth erupted from the surrounding water. Ponting and Captain Scott, who was a witness, both felt that he had been lucky to escape a nasty death as the whales were doing their best to tip him into the water. From the known habits of killer whales it seems that they were not acting aggressively but out of curiosity. It is also said that they catch penguins that have reached the apparent safety of the ice by tipping the floes over and that they use a similar trick to catch sleeping seals and baby walruses. Adult walruses are usually more than a match for a killer whale and they protect their young by carrying them on their backs, but Scammon tells us that a killer whale will come up under the parent, knocking it violently and tossing the youngster into the sea.

In view of the stories attached to the killer whale it is worth examining its diet in detail. No doubt it varies from place to place, as with other whales, but it is very likely that there has been an undue emphasis placed on the killer whale's predation on mammals. It is at seal colonies and whaling grounds that men will most often see killer whales, if only because that is where men gather to attack these animals themselves. The killer whales' more mundane fishing activities go unnoticed. In a study of killer whales caught in Japanese waters it was found that their main food is fish, principally cod and flatfish, and squid, in roughly equal numbers. The item next most frequently found in their stomachs was dolphins, followed by seals, octopus and finally sharks.

Although apparently unsensational, a diet of fish may have more serious consequences for man than all the slaughter of whales and seals. In 1952, bands of killer whales invaded the rich fishing grounds off south-west Iceland. They ate the fish and tore up the nets causing damage valued at tens of thousands of pounds. The Iceland government offered bounties on all killer whales destroyed and later equipped expeditions to hunt them, but with little effect. Finally, the United States Navy was asked to drop depth-charges on the whale packs. They only killed a few of the whales but the harassment was sufficient to drive the rest away to quieter, if poorer, feeding grounds.

6. Behaviour: Routine and Incredible

The success of any whale fishery is very largely dependent on knowing where to find whales. The sperm-whalers of the eighteenth and nineteenth centuries discovered by patient searching that there were several regions in both hemispheres where sperm whales might be found in large numbers. The true extent of their distribution was demonstrated by C. H. Townsend who painstakingly investigated and charted the capture of 36,908 sperm whales as recorded in the log books of American whalers between 1761 and 1920. He found that sperm whales are cosmopolitan but are grouped mainly in certain favoured areas, which had been the fishing grounds of the whalers. There was also some degree of movement, depending on the season, and the whalers often recorded groups of sperm whales that were obviously on migration. They were swimming in an apparently determined fashion along a compass course, and going too fast to be pursued.

From these observations and the results of the analysis of modern catches and marking experiments, a pattern of the movements of sperm whales has emerged. The majority spend most of their lives in tropical or warm seas, probably crossing the equator to get the benefit of the summer in each hemisphere. Only some of the males wander more widely and penetrate the cold waters of the Arctic and Antarctic.

The concentration of sperm whales on the main fishing grounds of the old whalers is due to an abundance of food in these areas. The squid on which they feed are particularly abundant where there is a meeting and mixing of warm and cool water. Hence important sperm-whaling grounds were located along the west coast of South America up to the equator, where the cool Humboldt Current runs northwards, and off the south-west coast of Africa which is influenced by the Benguela Current.

The migrations of whalebone whales (Figure 11) are more marked than those of sperm whales. They spend the summer months feeding on the rich supplies of crustaceans in polar waters then move to warm water nearer the equator to spend the winter where there is little, if any, food. The reason for the migrations seems to be twofold. The polar seas are extremely productive and during the summer months there are large accumulations of the planktonic crustaceans and molluscs on which whalebone whales feed. The whales gorge themselves during the short summer and then retreat, before the sea freezes and cuts off the food supply. They make their way to warmer regions, where there are few chances to feed and they have to survive on the

Northern Summer
and Southern Winter

Northern Winter
and Southern Summer

Feeding Grounds

Breeding Grounds

Breeding Grounds

Feeding Grounds

Figure 11 Outline of the migrations of whalebone whales (modified from Mackintosh).

reserves of blubber accumulated during the summer. During the winter courtship and birth takes place without the distraction of having to feed and, as the calves are born with little blubber, the warmer waters of temperate seas may make their early life considerably easier.

These migrations are as definite as those of geese flying to their Arctic nesting grounds or caribou threading their way through the Canadian forests to spend the summer on the tundra beyond. Schools of whales can be seen travelling north or south at certain times of the year and those species that migrate close to the shore, the right whales, the humpback and the gray whale, suffered particularly at the hands of hunters who could harry them in short forays from the shore.

Evidence that these migrations take place is conclusive; but very little is known about the routes taken, even for the coast-hugging species, and, with the exception of the Californian gray whale which breeds in lagoons, virtually nothing is known about the whereabouts of the summer breeding grounds. Now that the numbers of whalebone whales have been so much reduced by hunting the chances of tracing the migration routes and the breeding grounds are slight. It is not impossible that hunting has caused the whales to alter their itineraries and that their breeding grounds are sited well clear of the regular shipping lanes.

The study of migration has been most rewarding where the whales move almost in sight of land. The Californian gray whale leaves its feeding grounds in the Bering Sea some time in October and makes its way down 5,000 miles of coastline to Baja California. In March or April the return journey is made with the newborn calves. On the other side of the Pacific Ocean more gray whales will be swimming away from the region of Korea and passing up the Gulf of Tartary to the Sea of Okhotsk where they feed in isolation from their Californian cousins in the Bering Sea.

The separation of distinct populations on breeding and feeding grounds has been found in other whalebone whales. The southern populations of humpback whales are divided into five or six groups, as shown by recoveries of whale marks and observations on the movement of the whales. Each

Figure 12 The principal feeding grounds and migration routes of the humpback whale in the southern hemisphere.

group feeds in a fairly restricted zone of the Antarctic (see Figure 12) and migrates north to breeding grounds that are usually in shallow water. Migration is slow, for although individual whales swim at 5–6 knots, they seem to spend some time wandering about so that the overall movement north or south is very much slower. The speed of the whales is probably geared to fit with the needs of the annual cycle: arriving in the tropics in time to give birth and returning to the Antarctic after the ice has retreated. Nursing cows and their calves are the last to move south and the first to move north so they spend the least time in cold water.

Blue whales and fin whales are known to follow the pattern of movements of the whalebone whales, as summarized in Figure 11, but they spread out more on the feeding grounds. However, it seems that they, too, are divided into distinct populations so that wherever a whale wanders during the summer it returns to the same breeding grounds in winter. There are some exceptions and a few whales marked in one breeding ground have been recovered in another. As the southern winter is at the opposite time of year to the northern winter there is very little chance of whales from northern and southern populations intermingling around the equator but a few individuals end up in the wrong hemisphere. On the other hand, some whales stay in the polar regions all winter and do not take part in breeding.

The difficulty of following whales at sea has made it virtually impossible to study their social behaviour except during chance sightings when they may be seen doing something interesting. They may be encountered alone or in groups of varying numbers, but it is almost impossible to work out the composition of a school in terms of sex and age. The calves are the only category that can be easily distinguished, except in sperm whales where there is a size difference between sexes. Thus, it is not known whether groups of whales swimming close together and blowing in unison are proper social units, such as a family group, or merely the random gathering of a number of individuals.

Among the whalebone whales it seems most likely that schools are random gatherings. They consist of both sexes, although females with calves are more solitary, and when disturbed they may split up and rejoin in different combinations. A more definite social structure is seen in sperm whales where schools consist of cows with calves and one or more mature bulls, or of groups of young males. The size of the school is usually twenty to fifty but crowds of up to a hundred may gather on migration.

Social behaviour in any animal implies that individuals must be able to communicate in some way; and some form of communication is necessary to bring whales together in schools and to synchronize the behaviour of the members. Whales have long been known to make a variety of clicks, whistles and groans and the obvious assumption is that these are used in communication, although in recent years it has also been found that some cetacean sounds are used in echo-location. The recording of these calls has not been easy but the results have suggested that vocal communication by the whales may be very important.

Sperm whales have been heard emitting series of clicks, and analysis has shown that the clicks coming from one whale share certain characteristics of pitch and duration and that these characteristics differ in the clicks from another whale. In other words, each whale has an individual voice and, therefore, it is theoretically possible for sperm whales to identify each other by sound. What the whales tell each other is not known. The repetition of similar clicks can mean little in the way of a language and a whale is probably doing no more than monotonously indicating its position, like a radio beacon or lighthouse, so that its fellows know where it is and keep the school together.

More elaborate sounds have been recorded from fin whales and humpbacks. Roger Payne and his associates have recorded the calls of humpbacks as they pass Bermuda on their migration down the coast of America. The sounds of a humpback form a series of low pulses and tones that sweep up and down the scale. The series continues for many minutes but Dr Payne realized that the sounds fall into a pattern that is repeated and that the whales are singing like a bird: they are uttering a set sequence of sounds over and over in the form of a signature tune.

Each humpback appears to sing a personal tune by which it can be identified; but the function of the song is different from that of birdsong which is used to advertise the possession of a territory to potential rivals and mates. There is no proof, but it seems that the humpbacks are singing to keep track of each other and their utterances are better described as contact notes, the bird-watchers' name for the calls given by flocks of woodland birds to keep

4. Humpback whale inhaling as its 'blow' disperses. Note the knobs around the blowhole

5. Admission to the Whale Patter's Club. A minke whale surfaces at a small hole in the ice. The seals are crabeaters

6. The Whale Patter's Club treating a killer whale with respect. Note the distinctive white oval behind the eye

in touch as they forage among the foliage. Relatively speaking, a whale can see no further underwater than a bird can peer through the foliage but both can detect the sources of a sound. It has even been suggested that the excellent conduction of sound through water allows whales to hear each other over distances of hundreds of miles.

Merely swimming together in schools and calling to keep in touch is not evidence of a well developed social instinct but there is some indication, unfortunately very limited, that whales take notice of their companions and that they have social instincts that give them a high rank in the animal kingdom.

It is not uncommon for animals to come to the assistance of their young, and in whales the first parental duty is to raise a newborn calf to the surface for its first breath. The parents also react to their offspring's distress and sperm whales have been known to rescue injured calves by taking them in their mouths. Furthermore, it is not only the mother that reacts to a calf in distress. When a sperm whale calf was wounded by the propellor of the French research ship *Calypso*, a large number of adults were attracted to the scene by its distress calls.

Rescuing behaviour is not confined to assisting calves but is also elicited by injured adults. It is probably a very good indicator of a well developed social sense, as this behaviour is very rare even among the more intelligent land animals. There are several cases on record of both whalebone whales and toothed whales supporting injured companions at the surface. However, it is often asserted that, while males will come to the assistance of females, the latter will desert their mates.

Another form of co-operation among whales is shown by packs of killer whales which hunt together and are said to surround groups of seals or porpoises and cut off their retreat until they can single out a suitable victim. This leads to the most remarkable whale story of all time: the account of the co-operation between packs of killer whales and the whalers of Twofold Bay, in New South Wales. Friendly dolphins, like Opo of Opononi Beach near Auckland, New Zealand, have allowed people to ride on their backs and play with them, but the killer whales of Twofold Bay actually helped men to catch humpback whales. The killers were said to alert the whalers when a humpback appeared by leaping out of the water and splashing down. The

5

whalers would then launch a boat and chase after the humpback with the assistance of the killers, who tried to prevent it from sounding and even attempted to hinder its breathing by leaping on its blowhole. After the whale had been harpooned and despatched, the killer whales were allowed to remove the tongue and lips before the carcase was towed to the shore.

This story is recounted by Professor John Dakin in his book *Whalemen Adventurers* and he is at pains to explain that he was sceptical of the story at first, but that he interviewed several of the whalers who had formerly taken part in the co-operative hunts and was sufficiently impressed by their accounts to feel that the story had to be accepted. The intelligence displayed by cetaceans in marine aquaria and their co-operation with their keepers would suggest that it is not beyond the mental ability of killer whales to have behaved in such a way.

What is more surprising is that whales sometimes behave with apparent stupidity and allow themselves to get stranded on beaches, and, when rescued, to swim straight aground again. Some whales can survive stranding; gray whales sometimes voluntarily run aground, later floating free, and right whales have been seen close inshore amongst kelp, but for the majority, stranding means death. With the absence of a surrounding body of water the weight of the body presses on to weak ribs to make breathing difficult and overheating is also likely to occur. The main cause of death is by drowning when the tide returns to cover the blowhole before there is sufficient water to allow the whale to move.

It seems strange that whales should be caught in shallow water and beached. Some stranded whales have, on examination, proved to be diseased, or to have parasites in the cavities of the ear or in the central nervous system, which would put out of action any sonar mechanism. It has also been found that gently shelving beaches, where stranding always takes place, are not easily detected by shipborne sonar. A sick whale might easily overlook gently shoaling water and run aground. Unfortunately for this theory, whales in apparently perfect health sometimes strand. Is it, perhaps, that they are caught offguard, with their minds concentrated on other matters? For the moment, at least, this must remain as one of the many unsolved problems in the study of whales, as must the odd habit of whales coming straight back to the beach after they have been pulled off. In some cases this has happened during a mass stranding and it has been suggested that the whale is returning in response to distress signals being emitted by its comrades still on the beach. Yet whales that have stranded by themselves have sometimes deliberately swum back to the shore when dragged off.

7. Birth and Death

A discussion of the breeding habits of whales is necessarily brief because we have only the scantiest knowledge about their courtship and parental behaviour. The reason is the same as that which makes their migration routes and social behaviour poorly known: observations on the habits of whales have been mainly confined to sightings by the crews of whaling or merchant ships. They have been few because the whalebone whales breed in warmer waters during the time of the year that the whalers are back at home, and in areas away from the main shipping routes. However, now that dolphins are being bred in marine aquaria, the processes of mating and birth have been observed and it is probably allowable to assume that the same pattern of behaviour occurs in the large cetaceans.

By comparison, the physiology of the reproductive cycle, as opposed to breeding behaviour, has received considerable attention from the days of the *Discovery* expeditions onwards. As the carcases were being cut up by the whalers it was possible for zoologists to delve deep into the body cavity – at some risk to life and limb – and recover the reproductive organs. Apart from being drenched in blood from a cut artery, or buried under a cascade of entrails, the task is not as simple as a textbook dissection. As the dismembering of the whale proceeds, the organs get pulled out of their proper position and lost amongst the general upheaval while a relatively small organ, like a testis from a blue whale, can weigh 100 lbs and prove difficult to handle.

Examination of the reproductive organs reveals the stage of the reproductive cycle the whale had reached when it was killed. For males this means whether it was sexually active or not. The cycle in females is naturally more complex. Examination of the uterus shows whether the whale is pregnant, and at what stage; the mammary glands show whether it is nursing; and detailed examination of the ovaries will tell whether the whale was ready to breed again.

One practical drawback to these studies is that they can be carried out only at whaling stations. This means that the species that are not hunted have hardly been studied, and that nothing can be done outside the whaling season. Most of our knowledge is based on studies of fin whales and humpbacks, where hunting, and research, has been concentrated in the southern hemisphere during the summer, which is outside the breeding season. It is not even known where fin whales and the other rorquals breed. The Antarctic population appears to move up to about the latitude of Durban and may congregate in shallow water.

We have seen that whalebone whales migrate to warmer water in winter then return to feed in colder water during the summer. The purpose of these migrations, which in gray whales are about 5,000 miles each way, is to make use of the seasonal abundance of food during the summer, then to retire to warmer regions which are more favourable for the birth and early life of the young. Newborn whales lack the insulating layer of blubber that their elders possess, and would lose too much heat in the cold waters south of the Antarctic Convergence. As it is, mothers with calves migrate to the feeding grounds later than the other females and they, together with the males, keep to routes that take them through warmer water. Similarly, the calves are led away from the Antarctic before the end of the summer.

The two main events in the breeding of the Antarctic whales take place when the population is in its warm winter quarters. From calculations based on studies of their ovaries, it has been found that fin whales can mate all the year round. However, most of the calves are conceived between April and August, but what happens during mating is mostly a mystery. The actual act of mating takes only a few seconds and may take place with the whales lying horizontally or rearing vertically from the water, belly to belly. Prior to this there is considerable loveplay. Humpbacks have been seen caressing or slapping each other with their flippers, or gently swimming past one another with bodies touching. Prolonged loveplay is a feature of the mating of many mammals and in whales it is necessary because scent can play no part in telling the male whether or not the female is in breeding condition. He has to tell by her reactions to his advances.

If the mating is successful, and it is repeated several times, the female whale will carry a single embryo, rarely twins or triplets, down to the Antarctic. During her stay in the breeding grounds she will not have fed, and the embryo within her grows at a rate comparable with those of other mammals until she has been feeding for some time in the Antarctic. Then it starts to put on weight rapidly, at ten times the speed of a human baby. The acceleration may be due to the amount of reserves that the mother can now divert to the developing calf, but a fast growth rate is also essential for the calf to be ready for birth by the time that the mother returns to warmer water in the autumn.

The actual length of pregnancy has been estimated as $11\frac{1}{4}$ months for fin whales, and the other whalebone whales have pregnancies within the range of ten to twelve months. At birth a fin whale calf is twenty feet long; and a blue whale calf is twenty-five feet long and weighs over two tons, its growth from a fertilized egg in less than a year being the fastest rate of growth in the animal kingdom. These colossal babies are as much as one third or more of the mother's length but are only a fraction of her weight. No one has witnessed the birth of a whalebone whale but it must be presumed that they are born as in dolphins, tail first and with the flukes tucked in and the dorsal fin and flippers pressed against the body so that they do not catch.

The first action in any cetacean's life is to swim to the surface, perhaps with its mother's help, and take a gulp of air. The first breath is important, as it fills the lungs and corrects the buoyancy of the young animal. From then on it can swim well enough to keep up with its mother, keeping alongside her dorsal fin or by one of her flippers. A baby whale is less buoyant than an adult because it has very little blubber and this is part of the reason why it is comparatively light in weight for its length. Its dimensions are soon changed because it is fed on a particularly rich milk, three to four times more concentrated than cow's milk and said to taste of a mixture of fish, liver, milk of magnesia and oil. A revolting mixture to our taste but it obviously makes a very rich diet. The baby whale doubles its weight within a week and a young blue whale adds 200 lbs to its weight every day.

Suckling takes place underwater and the calf is force-fed, taking in a large quantity of milk before it has to surface for breath. The nipple lies in a slit in the mother's abdomen and the calf grabs it between the tongue and the roof of the mouth while milk is pumped in by contractions of muscles around the milk glands.

The mother whale does more than feed her calf. She is jealous of it, warding off other whales and going to its defence. Most of our knowledge of the breeding behaviour of the large whales concerns this last trait. It has been the cause of death or injury to many a whaler, when a whale with a calf has turned on her pursuers.

Charles Scammon, who wrote a very complete account of the gray whale and the methods of hunting it, gives many details of the behaviour of gray whales with calves. This species gives birth to its young in the shallow lagoons that fringe the coasts of California. In the middle of the nineteenth century whalers arrived each year to hunt them. They soon learnt that it was dangerous to harpoon a gray whale calf from an open boat. The enraged mother would attack the boat, butting it with her head or slapping it with her flukes. Despite this danger, the whalers preferred to hunt cows with calves because the cow had to keep to the slow pace of her offspring. They also traded on the whale's maternal instincts by harpooning the calf from the shore, towing it in and then harpooning the cow as she followed, helplessly, behind it.

Nowadays nursing cows and their calves of all whales are protected, although mistakes are made when the calf wanders from its mother's side. There is every likelihood that the pair of them will survive the period of nursing. In fin whales this lasts for six to seven months and the calf is weaned on its first visit to the Antarctic. This timing is no coincidence, as weaning takes place among the rich feeding grounds of the Southern Ocean. Learning to feed itself is a difficult stage in the life of any animal and it is an advantage for the learning period to come during a time of plenty.

By the time they are weaned the baby whales have approximately doubled in length; and the weight of a blue whale has shot up from two to twenty-three tons. The growth now slows down and at physical maturity, around thirteen to fifteen years, it almost ceases. By then blue whales are about eighty feet long and fin whales about ten feet shorter, with females being a few feet longer than males in both species.

The whalebone whales considered so far breed once every two years and the major events in the cycle fit the species' pattern of migration to and from the cold feeding grounds. Mating and birth take place in warm water where the adults subsist on their thick layers of blubber and weaning takes place in cold water where there is an abundance of food. In the toothed whales there is no regular north-south migration and cow sperm whales do not enter cold water. Their breeding cycle is accordingly not fitted in a biennial pattern. The same is also found in one whalebone whale, Bryde's whale, which is confined to warm water all the year round. It mates and gives birth at any season.

Sperm whales are polygamous, whereas whalebone whales appear to be monogamous. The male sperm whales fight amongst each other during the mating season and the victors apparently secure harems of females. The bachelors live in separate herds some of which travel into polar regions. Mating takes place in the spring and the pregnancy lasts sixteen months, as it does in killer whales as well, a considerably longer period than in whalebone whales. Lactation is also prolonged, lasting for about a year. Clearly the breeding of sperm whales does not conform to changing seasons and the length of the cycle means that they can breed only once in every three years.

Thereafter, however, the young sperm whales reach maturity at about the same age as whalebone whales, but there is one difference. Male sperm whales mature at a length of fifty feet but the females mature at forty feet. The larger size of the males is maintained throughout life and is probably linked with their habit of forming harems for mating. Similar size differences between the sexes are found in those species of seals in which the male holds a harem. The males of fur seals and elephant seals are far larger than the females, whereas there is little size difference between sexes in Weddell seals, common seals and others, where there is a loose social structure without much competition between the males.

Having considered the start of a whale's life it is natural to examine the other end of its lifespan. It used to be thought that whales were very longlived, merely because they were very large. There is no basis for a correlation between size and lifespan in animals, and it turns out that the life of a whale is not particularly long. A few fin whales have been found with earplugs that bear eighty laminae and may be around eighty years old but the average lifespan is more in the order of twenty-five to thirty years.

Before man discovered the means of slaughtering the great whales there must have been relatively stable populations of all species in which the birth-rate equalled the deathrate. We have seen that whales breed slowly, one calf every two or three years, so the deathrate must have been correspondingly low. As with most animals that have been studied, it is the young of the whales that are particularly vulnerable. They may be stillborn, or born with serious deformities that condemn them from the start, and they may not survive the period of learning to feed themselves. Furthermore, at this age they are more vulnerable to predation, by killer whales and sharks, and to disease and parasites.

Once fully grown, a whale faces few hazards. It will not suffer from severe climatic conditions except in the odd situation of being trapped by a frozen sea and prevented from blowing. This is an occurrence that is probably as rare as a mass stranding, but there is one record that shows that it is a distinct possibility. In 1957 a British exploring party was travelling down the frozen Crown Prince Gustav Channel, off the mainland of the Antarctic Peninsula. In one place they noticed a series of large pools in the ice through which a number of whales were blowing. There were several minke whales, one killer whale and one beaked whale. The explorers were able to stand at the edge of a pool and touch the whales as they came up. Thus the small and exclusive 'Pat-the-whale' Club was founded. A few weeks later the holes had shrunk to a few yards diameter and the fate of the whales seemed to be sealed. The explanation of this discovery is that the sea must have frozen across the head of the channel before the whales had a chance to move clear and they were only able to stave off drowning for as long as they could keep the vital breathing holes clear.

Stranding and being trapped by ice must count as fatal accidents that have little significant effect on the adult population. So, it would seem, is the role of predation which is limited to sporadic attacks by killer whales. There is one strange antagonist of whales, the swordfish. Blue whales have been found with the swords of swordfish buried deep in their bodies. The function of the sword is thought to be to kill fish for food but there are numerous records of swordfish ramming boats either by accident or deliberately. Attacks on whales must be for the same reasons, whatever they might be!

Ice traps and berserk swordfish make interesting tales, but they do not answer the question of what is the main cause of death among adult whales. Food supply is the important factor that limits the size of many animal populations and this may be the ultimate check on the numbers of whales. If new whales are continually being added to the population some must go short of food if the supply is not to become exhausted. Once an individual becomes undernourished it has to draw on its reserves and it will become weaker and less able to resist any further setback. Parasitic infections, injuries and diseases (of which cirrhosis of the liver, tuberculosis and pneumonia have been recorded) will then hasten the end.

The very old and very young whales are those that are particularly at risk from disease and starvation and it is deaths to these two categories that probably balance the population, if our knowledge of other animal populations is anything to go on. It is usual for animals to produce more young than are necessary for the maintenance of the species. The surplus die early and can be considered as a potential reserve that can perhaps survive and grow up if the numbers of adults drop. With the populations of some species of whales dropping to danger level through overhunting it is to be hoped that there is some means by which the maximum number of offspring can be brought to maturity and so bring about a rapid increase in numbers.

Part II

Whaling

'What do ye do when ye see a whale, men?'
'Sing out for him! . . . '
'And what do ye next, men?'
'Lower away, and after him'
'And what tune is it ye pull to, men?'
'A dead whale or a stove boat!'

'For God's sake, be economical with your lamps and candles! not a gallon you burn, but at least one drop of man's blood was spilled for it.'

HERMAN MELVILLE, *Moby Dick*

8. The Foundations of Whaling

The story of whaling starts before the beginning of history. The kind of whales hunted and the methods of hunting can only be guessed at, but as whaling developed it came to play an increasingly important part in the lives of maritime people. The whaling interests of different countries often clashed so that whalers needed the protection of arms. Nor were the whalers immune to outside events. The introduction of petroleum oil for lighting purposes, for example, hastened the eclipse of the sperm whale fishery, not long after the New England fleet had been almost completely destroyed in the American Civil War.

Although the production of whale-oil and whalebone were vital to the economy of many nations, whaling rarely, if ever, appears in their histories. In 1812 there was a war between Britain and America, yet, in British histories at least, the destruction of the American whaling fleets goes unrecorded. Perhaps this is because whaling appears to the historian as no more than another industry to provide the wealth and material whereby a nation can indulge in the more varied, dramatic and interesting spheres of domestic and foreign politics.

From Melville's quotations at the head of the chapter it would appear that whaling has a drama of its own; but the old whalers have left very scanty material on which to bring to life the day to day running of their profession. We know virtually nothing of how the Basque whalers operated in the sixteenth century and the situation improves only slightly over the years until William Scoresby Junior published his *Account of the Arctic Regions* in 1820. This contains the first full history and description of the whaling industry. Then, in 1874, Charles Scammon published an account of the American whale fishery. These two works contain factual descriptions of the methods of catching and processing whales in different parts of the world and they also give a very clear picture of life in whale ships, especially vivid in Scoresby's account of the various ways in which danger to life and limb can befall the crew.

The latter half of the eighteenth century and the first half of the nineteenth saw the heyday of the old-fashioned sperm-whaling in which rowing boats and hand harpoons were used for grappling with whales. This is the only phase of whaling that has become familiar through popular writing. It was immortalized by Herman Melville's *Moby Dick* which, although a work of fiction, is largely accurate in its background; for Melville himself had sailed in a whale ship. Nearly fifty years later in 1900 another masterpiece, Frank Bullen's *The Cruise of the Cachalot*, appeared. This is a true account of a voyage in the whale ship *Cachalot* that sailed around the world hunting over the same whale fishing grounds as Melville's ill-fated *Pequod*.

There are other accounts of such voyages, which lasted for three or four years and took their crews round the world, but the style is all too often that of the terse entries in a ship's log with little attempt at description. One of the most unusual narratives is that by Eliza Williams, wife of the captain of the New Bedford ship *Florida*. Whaling captains quite often took their wives to sea and Mrs Williams gave birth to two children during her first two-year voyage. In the same book, one of her sons continues the family's saga with a graphic account of the disaster that befell the American whaling fleet in 1871, and of a Pacific cruise undertaken when a boy.

The last story of the old time sperm-whaling is Robert Cushman Murphy's *Logbook for Grace*. This is the charming account, by one of America's foremost ornithologists, of a voyage in the brig *Daisy*, one of the last of the old-time sailing ships to be employed as a whaler. *Logbook for Grace* also forms a link with the present as the *Daisy* called in at South Georgia where the modern Antarctic whaling industry was being pioneered by C. A. Larsen. From this time onwards the whaling industry is swept up by the modern development of documentation. Each year sees published statistics of whales caught, their products and their value; scientific studies on the habits of whales and the food value of their flesh are poured out; while popular articles and books appear, describing whaling adventures or condemning the rapacity of an industry that is killing off the whales faster than they can breed. There is, however, no modern equivalent of Melville or Bullen, although F. D. Ommaney perhaps gives us the equivalent of *Logbook for Grace* in his *South Latitude*.

The whaling industry has sprung up independently in many parts of the world at many different times and this makes an account of its development anything but straightforward. However, it becomes clear from both historical and narrative accounts of whaling that wherever whaling has been carried out as an organized industry its progress has followed a regular, although very general, pattern.

At first, catching of whales is comparatively easy because of their abundance and their habit of swimming close to the shore. Hunters flock after them and there is no difficulty in finding sponsors for whaling expeditions as the sale of whale products becomes an important part of the economy. Handsome profits can be made but gradually the whale populations are hunted out and the whalers are forced farther afield in search of new stocks. This trend continues until so few whales are left that the industry becomes unprofitable and collapses, perhaps leaving a remnant to eke a living out of the remaining stocks. Occasionally there is a slight recovery of the industry as the whale population revives.

There are two main variations on this pattern. The industry may never expand; in fact it may never really become an industry, as in the case of whaling by coastal people such as the Faeroese and Eskimos. They catch whales for the immediate use of the community in much the same way as the Eskimos hunt seals and game animals: for food, clothing and other domestic purposes. In such cases the number of whales killed does not seriously affect the stocks and whaling continues according to the traditional pattern until halted for economic reasons, such as increased affluence of the hunters.

Advanced whaling industries may close down before the whale stocks are exhausted, through political or economical difficulties. The New England sperm-whaling, for instance, received severe blows from both causes. Many whaling vessels were destroyed during the Civil War, then mineral oil was discovered in 1859 and whale-oil was pushed out of the market for fuel and lubricating oils. Nevertheless, in line with the general pattern, sperm-whalers continued to sail from New England ports until 1925 and transplanted offshoots of the industry still linger in the Azores and Madeira.

Another pattern that emerges from the history of whaling is seen in the techniques used. This is not surprising when one considers that, except for primitive peoples who exploited whales mainly as food, whales have been caught principally for the oil in their blubber. Thus whaling always involves three basic processes: 1) capturing and killing, 2) stripping the blubber and 3) extracting oil from the blubber. The methods used in each process have developed along similar lines wherever whaling has flourished. Even the modern whaling of the twentieth century follows the same plan. Its output and efficiency have been changed by the addition of machinery in the same way that the English cotton industry was changed by the Industrial Revolution.

Until harpoons with explosive heads were invented, the capturing and killing of a whale were separate operations. The former involved the use of a harpoon, a barbed spear that caught fast in the whale's flesh. A line from the harpoon to the whalers' boat, or to floats, impeded the whale's movements so that it tired sufficiently for the whalers to close with it and attack with long, razor-sharp lances. Once dead, the whale was towed to the shore, or to the whalers' ship, where it was stripped of its blubber and other valuable parts such as whalebone, or the teeth in the case of sperm whales and, latterly, meat and endocrine organs. This mammoth dissection, known to the American whalers as 'cutting-in', was a skilled as well as an arduous and often dangerous job. The large slabs of blubber were then cut into small pieces and 'tried-out', that is cooked in large cauldrons to express the oil from the tissue of the blubber.

This, then, is the outline of the course and techniques of the whaling industry. The origins of each are, however, lost because man first started to hunt whales in prehistoric times. There is no doubt that the first whales to be exploited were those that were unfortunate enough to be stranded. The discovery of a school of dolphins or a single rorqual cast up on the beach must have represented a major windfall to primitive man who, judging by the habits of some of the aboriginal hunting and gathering tribes of today, probably paid little attention to storing food but never lost the opportunity of gorging themselves until sated.

The earliest evidence of men deliberately seeking out and killing whales lies in a few drawings scratched on rock faces in Norway. One, estimated to be 4,000 years old, was found on the island of Røddøy in northern Norway. It depicts a man in a boat, a seal and two porpoises. There is also an elk which does not fit in the rest of the picture; but a similar confusion of animals, often painted at different times, is found in the much older cave-paintings at Lascaux. Another picture, at Meling, shows a whale surrounded by boats filled with men, one of which appears to have been upset by the whale's tail, a scene often shown in illustrations of whaling.

These pictures may be idle doodles scratched for fun, as in the case of some modern rock paintings in Africa and Australia, or part of a ritual of sympathetic magic, in which the painting or scratching of an image is sup-posed to assist in hunting the real animal, but it seems reasonable to suppose that the early Norwegians actively hunted the cetaceans they then drew.

Unfortunately, none of these rock carvings show the manner in which these whales were secured but, from our knowledge of whaling in historic times, two ways seem likely. The hunters of the north-west Pacific, living in the Aleutian and Kurile Islands, Kamchatka and Hokkaido, pursued large whales in one-man kayaks, as in the Røddøy picture. The whales, usually humpbacks, were attacked with spears tipped with a poison extracted from the roots of aconite, and left to die. Several days later the corpse would be washed up on the shore and the owners identified by the marks on the spear. The whale was then divided between the people who killed it and those who found it.

Primitive harpooning of whales was carried out by Indians and Eskimos on both coasts of North America at least until the nineteenth century. Singly, or in groups, the hunters pursued the whales, thrusting harpoons into their backs. Attached to the harpoons were floats of sealskin or wood which resisted the whale's progress as it sounded, tiring it and revealing its position to the waiting hunters. As soon as the hunters could get near, the whale was speared, again and again, until it was dead.

Scammon records that the Indians of the north-east Pacific hunted gray whales in fleets of canoes, each carrying a crew of eight. When a whale was killed it was towed back to the village and divided up to provide a feast for the whole community, with the surplus oil being sold to tribes from the interior. In the same way as the Indians of the great plains and northern forests utilized every part of bison and caribou carcases, so the coastal Indians and Eskimos had many uses for their whales. The whalebone was used for sledge runners and the Eskimos of North Greenland relish squares of blubber and skin cut from newly killed narwhals. Known as *mattak*, the skin has a nutty flavour and is particularly rich in vitamins.

Perhaps the most hazardous method of whaling ever practised was the almost suicidal technique recorded of certain South American Indians. The whale was chased by canoe until one man could leap on to its back and thrust a sharpened stake into its blowholes. If the operation was successful the whale suffocated.

Around the coast of northern Europe there has long been practised another method of catching whales whose origin extends back into pre-history. It probably developed later than the spearing and harpooning of whales just described because, to be successful, it requires the co-operation of a community with elaborate conventions and signalling systems. This is the deliberate driving of a school of whales on to the shore where they can be slaughtered. The species captured is the pilot whale which lives in schools of hundreds and sometimes thousands.

The whole school becomes stranded easily because of a strong herd instinct which leads to the school swimming into shallow water and on to the shore if one or more of their number becomes stranded – perhaps in response to distress signals. The technique is for the hunters to form a semicircle of boats behind the school and gently guide it towards a convenient beach. When the school is nearly aground one whale is lanced. Panicking, it races shorewards and the rest follow blindly rather than turning and breaking through the cordon of boats.

In the Faeroe Islands where it is known as *grindadrap* – the killing of the *grind* or school – records of pilot-whaling date back to 1584. It also used to take place in the Hebridean, Orkney and Shetland Islands where it was known as 'caaing'. As all these island groups were peopled by Norse settlers it seems reasonable to suppose that the custom originated along the coast of Norway where the narrow, steep-walled fjords would have eased the task of shepherding a school of whales. The importance of pilot-whaling to the communities of these rather barren islands is shown by the proportion of the Faeroese law books which is taken up with legislature concerning the *grinda-*

drap and the zeal with which the Faeroese show towards the exercise even today. The most graphic description of Faeroese pilot-whaling is to be found in Kenneth Williamson's *The Atlantic Islands*.

The school of pilot whales is sighted from the shore or from a boat. If the latter, a makeshift flag is waved to alert other boats and people on the shore. Immediately the alarm – the *Grindaboð* – is raised and every available person rushes, by car, cart or foot, to the harbour. School children are released for the day, and the only people not welcomed are pregnant women because both in Faeroe and Shetland it was thought that their presence on the beach prevented the whales from landing. Meanwhile the message is passed to other parts of the countryside, originally by a network of messengers and beacons, but now by telephone messages that have priority over all other calls.

The whale school becomes the rallying point for the boats which are placed under the leadership of a captain, whose job is to direct the coaxing of the whales into a harbour. The chosen harbour must have a gently shelving shore of mud or sand on which the whales will be easily stranded. It is selected after a consideration of various factors. For instance, pilot whales prefer to move into the wind so the nearest harbour may not be chosen if it is downwind of the school. It may even be necessary to corral the whales in a cove until conditions become more favourable.

The boatmen take care not to frighten the whales but gently chivvy them along by dropping into the sea white-painted stones to which lines are attached. As the school nears the beach the captain gives the word and one whale is lanced in the tail so that it springs towards the beach. Its companions follow and the slaughter starts as men thrust at the whales with lances and knives from the boats or jump overboard to tangle with them at close quarters. At the same time other men wade out from the shore to assist, stabbing at the threshing bodies or planting hooks into them so that they can be dragged ashore by the waiting crowd, while children run underfoot slicing at the bodies.

When the carnage is over it is the turn of the officials, the *metaringarmenn*, who divide the catch using traditional Norse tallies. The distribution of the meat and blubber follows strict rules as laid down by law, although these have been altered to fit modern conditions. The largest whale is given to the boat that first sighted the school, a portion is sold to reimburse men whose gear has been damaged, another portion is used to pay the *metaringarmenn* and other officials, some meat is put aside for the feast that follows and the rest is divided amongst the community. Some fresh meat is boiled but most is dried or salted for winter use. The heart, liver, lips and kidneys are fried and little is discarded except the head and flippers.

In Shetland, the practices were rather different. Except in times of famine only the blubber was used, being sold to merchants, often in exchange for spirits. Perhaps this is why pilot-whaling was less important to the Shet-landers. They also received less of the proceeds, as two-thirds of the catch went to the Admiral of the County and the landowner where the whales came ashore. The last Shetland 'caa' was held in 1903, and pilot whales are now rarely seen off Shetland, but a similar practice still survives on the other side of the world where Solomon Islanders drive schools of porpoises ashore. The porpoises are kept on the move by one man in each boat, clashing stones together underwater, and when they reach the beach they are dragged ashore by the hundreds of islanders that have gathered there. The meat is eaten and the teeth are used as money for buying wives. A necklace of a thousand teeth worth about £25, being the value of a bride.

The killing of schools of whales by Faeroese and Solomon Islanders is more than a slaughterhouse operation, providing food and products for trade. There is the thrill of the hunt, so common in both primitive and civilized communities, culminating in an outburst of blood lust. In Faeroe there are wild celebrations following the division of the catch and foreigners are sometimes warned to stay indoors. J. G. Millais conveys the universal excitement through an anecdote in which a Shetland preacher noticed that members of his flock were furtively stealing away, as word of the arrival of whales spread. He hurriedly wound up his sermon with the words 'Let us all have a fair start – just a fair start' and joined the exodus from his church.

Pilot-whaling is also carried out at the present time in Trinity Bay, Newfoundland, where the whales are driven into narrow fjords and imprisoned behind a net. The capture lacks the traditions and excitement of the Faeroes or the Solomon Islands and the carcases are used for a more prosaic purpose; as food for ranch-bred mink.

In Newfoundland 3,000–4,000 whales may be caught each year and at one time the Faeroese averaged about four hundred a year but whale stranding has also been practised elsewhere on a casual basis. In 1959, a whalebone whale was driven ashore in eastern India by the crews of two fishing boats and dragged up the beach by one hundred and fifty men. The blubber fetched little money but an enclosure was built around the whale and between fifteen and twenty thousand people paid 2,000 rupees (£150) to see it. During the four days that the whale was on exhibition it was perfumed with agarbathis, frankincense and mothballs.

If the two oldest methods of capturing whales are to drive them ashore or to harpoon them, it seems that the latter is the more practicable because it requires fewer men and less time than the shepherding of a school or an individual whale. It is the harpooning and spearing of whales that was developed by the mediaeval Basques into the organized industry which became the foundation of all later industries, including the worldwide sperm-whaling of the eighteenth and nineteenth centuries and the Antarctic whaling of the present day.

The Basques are generally regarded as the Fathers of Whaling; they later taught the secrets of their trade to the English, Dutch and other nationalities; but there is evidence that the Basques, in turn, learned whaling techniques from Norwegians, who, as Normans, settled around the Bay of Biscay.

The first written record of Norwegian whaling appears in an account of a sea journey around Norway to the White Sea, given by a Norwegian, Ottar or Ohthere to King Alfred of Wessex in about the year 890. Ohthere met whalers, but Alfred does not record what whales were hunted or how they were caught except that Ohthere and five companions had killed sixty in two days. The whales were 48-50 ells long and they could have been whalebone whales, if the Norwegian ell is taken as being approximately one English foot. The two likely species are the Biscayan right whale, which was later hunted by the Basques, or the gray whale. The latter is now extinct in the Atlantic, but its skeleton has been found in the Zuider Zee and there is good evidence that it was once hunted in Icelandic waters and still occurred along the coasts of eastern America in the eighteenth century.

Early Norwegian whalers have also been credited with inventing a giant crossbow or ballista for use as a harpoon gun, but this may be due to confusion with the use of a crossbow that survived in some Norwegian fjords until recently. When a whale was found in a suitably narrow fjord, its escape was cut off by a line of nets and rusty, dirty crossbow bolts were fired into its back. In due course it died of septicaemia and was hauled out on to a beach.

However, the Norwegians fade out from the mainstream of whaling history until the second half of the nineteenth century when Svend Føyn's invention of the first really practical harpoon gun revolutionized whaling and paved the way for the twentieth century mechanized whaling. This was dominated first by the Norwegians and, recently, by the Japanese. The mediaeval Japanese had already developed whaling techniques, independently of the West but following the same pattern, and producing what must be the oldest heavy industry with production line methods. In due course they learned the methods that were being developed by Western countries and are now one of the leading whaling nations.

9. The Development of an Industry

Today, Biarritz, St Jean-de-Luz and St Sebastian are seaside towns made famous as spas or watering places in the early part of this century. Yet these three towns, together with others around the south-east corner of the Bay of Biscay, were the home of the first organized whaling industry. Previously, whales had been caught mainly for the immediate benefit of the local community, but here in the Basque provinces of Spain and France, whale products became important items of trade.

The Basques probably started to hunt whales in the tenth century but by the twelfth century their industry was firmly established and it remained so for at least four hundred years. The important part that whaling played in the life of the Basque ports is shown by the number that have whales on their coats of arms and by the importance which kings attached to them. At Guetaria the first whale of the season was given to the king, presumably in the form of the cash it realized, rather than as an actual carcase, and at Zaruaz the king received a long slice of meat from the back of each whale caught.

At this time the western coast of France was in English hands and the English kings taxed all whales brought into Biarritz. In fact, the kings of England were awarded the title of Honorary Harpooner and in 1324 the statute *De Praerogativa Regis* declared whales to be royal fish and therefore the property of the Crown. This royal prerogative fell into disuse many years ago, but it was only in 1970 that a move was taken to abolish it as an inconvenient relic of the past. It was pointed out that several tons of whale rotting on a holiday beach is a public nuisance, if not a health hazard, and it is inconvenient to have to seek royal assent to its removal. This move was eventually defeated on the grounds that the machinery of reporting carcases enabled the British Museum (Natural History) to obtain many valuable specimens of whales which would otherwise be lost.

The whales hunted by the Basques were mainly Biscayan right whales, then abounding in large herds whose migration routes led them close inshore. Right whales are so called because they are the right whales to hunt from small boats. They travel slowly and even when hurrying cannot outpace small rowing or sailing boats. Equally important, they do not sink when killed so that it is possible for the small boats to tow carcases back to the shore.

The most valuable products of the right whales were the blubber, which was rendered into oil for lighting purposes, and the whalebone or baleen. Whalebone had a variety of uses which were based on two important properties. It is stiff yet elastic and when immersed in hot water it becomes pliable and can be moulded. This made it an excellent material for corsets, fishing rods, whips, sweeps' brushes, the seats of chairs, springs in machinery and so on. In the seventeenth century whalebone was worth as much as £2,250 per ton and the whalebone from one whale made a whaling cruise profitable, but it has since been superseded by spring steel and plastics and, nowadays, when the maximum profit is squeezed out of each whale, the whalebone is the only part to be discarded; although a little is used for making brooms and riding crops.

There is no contemporary description of how the Basques caught their whales but we can get a good idea by deduction from what little information exists. Whaling was probably a joint enterprise carried out by the community on the Faeroese pattern, as shown by the remains of look-out towers from which a watch was kept for whales and by the way the catch was divided. In Lequeitio, for instance, the whalebone from each whale was divided into three parts; one part to cover costs for repairing the church and two parts for repairing the harbour.

The town seal of Biarritz, dated 1351, shows a small boat approaching a whale. Three of the crew are rowing or paddling, one is working a steering oar and the fifth is standing in the bows with a harpoon at the ready. So even in this stylized portrayal we see an arrangement similar to that used by the American sperm-whalers and British right-whalers of the eighteenth and nineteenth centuries. This is only to be expected, as the English and other European whalers were taught by the Basques who sailed on their whaling ships.

The word harpoon is said to come from the Basque *arpoi* but this has probably been derived from the French *harper* – to seize or grapple – which may in turn have come from the Latin *harpago* – a hook or grappling iron. Sir Clements Markham who travelled through the Basque provinces in search of whaling relics found a harpoon with a movable barb that was held closed by a ring. As the harpoon entered the whale's body the ring was pushed back and the barb allowed to open and grip the flesh. Similar harpoons were once used by the Norwegians in hunting belugas, and this is further evidence for a link between them and the Basques. Movable barb harpoons must, however, have been abandoned at some stage in the mainstream of whaling history because fixed barb harpoons were later in general use until the toggle-iron was invented by an American blacksmith in 1848, although Eskimos also invented a form of movable barb harpoon.

The number of whales killed by the Basques does not seem to have been very great. In the sixteenth century the men of Lequeitio killed, on average, only one or two whales a year, but in 1538 they killed six whales. Compared with the numbers killed in modern whaling (about 60,000 whales were killed each year during the 1950's), the Basques would seem to have taken a negligible number of whales, but during the middle of the seventeenth century the catches decreased and right whales became rare along the Biscayan coast.

We have no idea how abundant were the Biscayan right whales when the Basques started their operations, but it is surprising that such a comparatively small industry could have so severely affected their numbers. It is not impossible that over the course of three or four centuries the whales learned to avoid the coasts and took to a new route farther out to sea.

Until the modern whaling fleets started to scour the oceans and kill whales by the thousand, it was often suggested that the decreasing success of a particular fishery was due to the whales changing their habits. Melville appeared to be convinced that sperm whales were not decreasing in numbers but had changed their habits. He claimed that at one time they lived solitarily or in small schools but, under pressure of hunting, banded in very large, but well scattered, caravans and so were less frequently encountered. Scammon describes how the gray whales started giving the shores of California a wide berth a few years after intensive whaling started there.

Whatever the cause of the whales' disappearance from the Bay of Biscay, the Basque whalers had to travel farther afield, although porpoises and the occasional right whale were killed in the Bay of Biscay until the late nineteenth century. In the sixteenth century Basques and others were fishing for cod on the Grand Banks off Newfoundland and the news soon spread that there was an abundance of whales there. The Basque whalers were quick to take advantage of the new whale-fishing ground and in 1578 Anthony Parkhurst recorded seeing twenty to thirty Basque whaling ships off Newfoundland.

This was the period that western Europeans started to thrust out across the Atlantic in voyages of discovery. Starting with Columbus' voyage to the New World in 1492, the Portuguese and Spanish followed towards the warmer regions of the Caribbean and South America to find a passage to India and China. At the same time the northern nations were sending expeditions in search of the North-west Passage to the same destination. Sebastian Cabot set out from Bristol and reached Labrador in 1496 and attempted to find the North-west Passage in 1517. He was followed by the Englishman Jonas Poole (in 1583) and John Davis (in 1585). In 1596 the Dutch explorer Barendz discovered Spitzbergen and Hudson sailed into the bay that carries his name in 1610. The North-west Passage was not finally revealed until 1850 but, as the Portuguese and Spaniards discovered the riches of tropical America, so the English and Dutch explorers came home with stories of seas infested with whales. These were Greenland right whales and entrepreneurs of both countries, together with Danes, Germans and others, soon set sail to the northern seas, where fortunes were made, lives lost and adventures experienced, the equal of those recounted from the better known and warmer climate of tropical America.

At first, the key to success at whaling lay in hiring Basques to perform the duties of catching and cutting up the whales, but these pioneers disappeared from the scene as their employers learnt to do the intricate tasks themselves. The ships used in these voyages were only 100–200 feet long and carried crews of up to fifty. Richard Hakluyt gives advice on the fitting out of a whaling-ship in his *Collection of Voyages*. Among the more noteworthy items to be carried are 150 hogsheads (9,600 gallons) of cider, 4 tunnes (1,024 gallons) of wine, 4½ kintals of bread for each man, as well as harping irons (harpoons), javelins – great and small, tackles, hooks, hogsheads, kettles, furnaces 'to melt the Whale in', ladles, '3 pairs of boots great and strong, for them that shall cut the Whale' and five 'pinnases' (pinnaces). The crew should include 'five men to strike with harping irons [one for each "pinnase"], two cutters of whale, five coopers and a purser or two'. The 'cutters of whale', known as specksioneers from the Dutch *Specksynder* – fat-cutter, were important men and later became the chief harpooners as well as overseers of the processing of the carcase, but the office eventually lapsed.

The first English ship to go whaling in the Arctic seas, as opposed to the rather warmer seas of Newfoundland and Iceland, set out from Hull in 1611. It had a profitable voyage and more ships followed in later years. In 1612 Dutch ships joined in the chase and the two countries were rivals for the next two hundred years, with the Dutch leading at first but eventually losing out as England became dominant both economically and politically. This was a golden age of whaling, perhaps rivalled only by the early years of Antarctic whaling where there were similar vast schools of whales to be had for the taking. It was the time when whalebone fetched the oft-quoted price of £2,250 a ton and each whale yielded $1\frac{1}{2}$ tons of whalebone and 25 tons of oil.

The seventeenth-century whalers worked around the coasts of Jan Mayen and Spitzbergen and this was known as the Greenland fishery, Spitzbergen then being known as East Greenland. There was considerable rivalry among the whalers until it was realized that there were enough whales for all. The Muscovy Company, a body of merchants similar to the Hudson's Bay Company but trading with Russia, sent ships around the North Cape into the White Sea and obtained a royal charter granting monopoly of the whaling rights in northern waters. This was challenged by other English companies as well as by foreigners, and considerable effort and money were wasted in sending armed ships to protect the whalers. Eventually it was realized that there was room for all and the coast of Spitzbergen was divided between the interested nations.

The profits from the Greenland fishery could be enormous; one whale paid for outfitting a ship and a ship might catch over fifty whales in a season, sometimes abandoning the carcases through lack of space or time. On the other hand, ships sometimes came home empty or failed to return altogether. Again, their cargo and equipment might be forcibly removed by ships of another nation because monopolies or the division of the coastline were only effective when supported by power. Sometimes the English came back rich and sometimes the Dutch or French were winners. Occasionally insult was added to injury as when an English captain complained that one Cornelius de Cock said that 'our King of England was a Scotchman, and that his picture stood at Flushinge with an emptie purse by his side'. The English seem to have been generally unpopular as they ignored the unwritten 'Greenland Law' – that a whale belonged solely to the ship that was fastened to it – and behaved 'as Lords of the Ocean and all its inhabitants'.

A handful of accounts of Greenland whaling appeared during the seventeenth century. The procedures that they describe had already been established for up to five centuries, having been learned from the Basques and, apart from the quaint language used, the authors could have been sailing in the same ships as Melville, Bullen or Murphy. A high degree of efficiency in the use of rowing boats, hand harpoons and lances for the killing of whales must therefore have been attained at an early stage in the history of whaling and there was almost no way in which it could be improved until the introduction of harpoon guns and steam catchers.

In 1671 Frederic Marten set sail for Spitzbergen in the whale-ship *Jonas in the Whale*. On his arrival at the whaling-grounds he saw many ships which when passing 'hailed one another, crying *Holla!* and asked each other how many fish they had caught'. This was another area in which the English earned the scorn of other nations. It was their habit to ask the other crew how many whales they had caught, then to claim a total two or three in excess of the other's. The habit of 'speaking a ship' or 'gamming' became a convention with whalers and in the nineteenth century two ships might heave-to while the crews went aboard each others' ships to chat and compare adventures. Except for the rare call at a port for stores or repairs, gamming was the only contact the whalers might have with the outside world for three or four years on end.

The whalers that Frederic Marten observed were chasing their quarry in boats that held six men: a harpooner, a steersman and four oarsmen. They rowed up to the whale, the harpooner stood up and thrust his weapon into the whale's back. The harpoon had two tines, each with a sharp leading edge but blunt behind like an axehead, so that it cut easily into the whale's flesh but would not pull out. The harpoon was not intended to kill or even disable the whale, but merely fastened it to the boat. When it struck the whale's back the heavy wooden shaft came away, leaving a fore-runner of the best pliable hemp rope running back to the boat where it was fastened to coils of heavier, tarred rope.

As soon as the whale was harpooned, or 'struck', the oarsmen slipped their oars and turned to face the bow. Great care was taken as the line rushed out to see that it ran freely without kinks or loops that might catch and that it ran straight over the bows so that the boat was not pulled over. In the centre of the boat was a stout post, the stave, later known as the bollard or, to the Americans, the loggerhead. The line passed around the stave to slow its running, the friction being so great that it had to be continually dampened with sea water to prevent the wood scorching.

By slowing the rate at which the whale drew out the line through wrapping it around the stave and hauling in any slack, the boat was gradually drawn towards the whale giving the harpooner a chance to kill it with lance-thrusts. The lances were six foot steel rods, tipped with sharp blades and fitted into a twelve-foot wooden shaft. As soon as the boat closed with the whale the harpooner thrust the lance into its body, worked it about, churning and plunging to enlarge the wound and strike a vital spot. His aim was to place the lance into the whale's back and to penetrate the great blood vessels, causing the whale to spout blood, a sure sign that its end was near.

With the thrashing of the whale in its agony and the movement of the boat the harpooner had little chance to aim and place the lance where he wanted. He had to stab as and when he could, calling out to his crew to row forward to the whale or back quickly to avoid the lashing flukes, while the steersman manipulated the long steering oar, spinning the boat to keep the bow towards the whale.

The physical and mental stress on the boat's crew can be imagined. Firstly, they spent hours in an open boat on the icy sea, because there might be anything from fifteen minutes to forty hours between the harpooning and the killing of a whale. They might be towed out of sight of their parent ship and be lost as darkness or fog enveloped them. Then, over and above such discomforts that can befall any mariner, their main aim was to bring their boat as close as possible to one of the largest animals that has ever existed and repeatedly wound it.

The whalers must have been continually conscious that every inch of harpoon line hauled back into the boat brought them nearer the danger of the stricken whale. William Scoresby summed up this danger in a letter to Sir Joseph Banks:

> In the Tail lays the whole strength of the whale, it is the fisherman's [whaler's] greatest fear, the power and the weight so great that boats are stove, upset, perhaps completely severed in two, sometimes thrown quite out of the water, or crushed to atoms beneath the stroke. The Tyro shrinks with fear, and views with terror the mighty member waving above his head, and cracking like a whip but 10 times louder which sometimes tempts him to leap into the sea to seek refuge from the impending blow.

It is incredible that men should have pitted themselves against these monstrous creatures with such frail equipment and at such close quarters. Rarely has man taken on fights with animals at such heavy odds. It calls to mind knights errant charging fiery dragons or Masai warriors grabbing the tails of lions while their companions attack with spears, but the knights and warriors battled for honour and prestige while whalers toiled for a low wage. The most that a whaleman could hope for when his boat was wrecked was that he might be picked up, shocked and frozen, by another boat.

It was the custom for the other crews to wait nearby and lend extra lines if the whale was pulling strongly (one whale is recorded as pulling out over 10,000 yards of line) and to help tow the carcase back. For the killing of the whale was not the end of the operation, the tail had to be cut off or lashed up to make towing easier and the carcase laboriously rowed back to the ship where it had to be cut up before the weather deteriorated or the body decayed.

It is hard to find out just how hazardous was the catching of whales from open boats. Danger was always present but luck and skill must have lessened the risk or whaling would never have been a worthwhile proposition. Between 1669 and 1778 the Dutch whalers lost about four per cent of their men which, considering the hazards to life in those days, does not seem to be particularly high.

In the early years of the Greenland whale-fishery the ships operated close inshore. The whales were towed to the shore where each nation had set up a factory for stripping the carcases of their blubber and whalebone. In 1622 the

Dutch constructed the 'village' of Smeerenburg (Dutch *smeeren* – to melt, *burg* – town), sending building materials out from Holland and erecting a cluster of huts behind the shore. Smeerenburg soon expanded into an Arctic metropolis. Each whaling company had its own slipway, boilers and warehouses and there was accommodation for upwards of 15,000 men. In the wake of the whalers came tradesmen to sell tobacco, spirits and fresh bread, and there was even a church and a fort.

The business of boiling, or trying-out, the blubber was conducted on the production-line principle. As the blubber was hauled ashore any remaining pieces of flesh were stripped off by the waterside man, who stood up to his knees in the sea. He also cut the strips of blubber into lumps weighing about 200 lbs. Each lump was carried up the shore by wheelbarrow and cut into smaller pieces which were placed on a chopping block made of the tough flesh of a whale's flukes and sliced into fine shreds. These were put into a large copper boiler mounted on a brick furnace – the tryworks. The blubber was heated and the mixture of oil and tissue that results was put through a sieve and the oil poured into a series of three vats half full of water to cool. The vats were mounted at different levels and were connected by spouts so that the oil ran from the top vat to the bottom vat, being progressively cooled, while impurities sank into the water. Meanwhile the jaws of the whale were stripped of their whalebone, each blade being scrubbed with sand and scraped to remove the tissue that secured it in the gum.

The thick, viscid oil retrieved from the blubber was called train-oil (from the Dutch *traan* – a tear or drop). It was used for lighting, as a lubricant and, as manufacturing advanced, in the manufacture of soap and paint and the processing of jute. Glycerine was extracted to make explosives and in the early nineteenth century several English towns were lit by gas made from train-oil. The oil and whalebone were sent home in barrels either in the whale-ships or, when the Spitzbergen whaling was at its peak, in merchant ships that came out in ballast.

The height of the Spitzbergen inshore or bay whaling came about 1636. After that catches declined as the whales either became scarce or changed their habits. The whale-ships had then to pursue them out at sea or among the pack ice. The splash and hiss of the waves breaking over the ice floes drowned the noise of the approaching boats and made stalking the whales easier, but the ice floes brought a new hazard for the whalers because a harpooned whale might try to escape by swimming under them. The harpooner had an awkward decision to make if this happened because, to save his boat, he had to cut his line thereby losing not only the whale but also his harpoon and many yards of rope. One trick, unpleasant for the crew, was to leave the line fastened to the boat, jump into the sea and wait to be picked up by another boat. The whale had then to tow the boat as well as the rope – which even by itself has a surprising resistance to being dragged through the water. Eventually, it was hoped, the whale would die and the boat would act as a buoy to mark its position.

During the second half of the seventeenth century Smeerenburg and the other shore stations declined in importance because the distance that the whales had to be towed became too great. The blubber was now stripped while the whale lay alongside the ship and was cut up and stored in barrels on board. The blubber was tried-out at a shore station or kept in the barrels until the return home.

A few French ships were fitted out with tryworks on the deck so that the blubber could be boiled at sea but too many ships caught fire for the practice to become popular. Blubber continued to be brought back to Europe in barrels and, later, in iron tanks until the nineteenth century, despite the fact that the Americans successfully used shipboard tryworks when sperm-whaling in the tropics and hunting in the North Pacific and Bering Sea.

Flensing a whale alongside a ship was a difficult task, particularly if the sea was rough. The whale was tied to the side of the ship, head facing sternwards, on the port side. Two boats were moored outside the whale to act as a platform from which the specksioneer or harpooners cut great furrows in the blubber with long handled knives. If there was a sea running, the movement of the ship, whale and boats made the operation precarious and the men often wore spiked boots to give them a firm grip on the slippery skin of the whale.

The whale lay on its side during this operation and large rectangles of blubber, each weighing about a ton, were lifted from the body. The harpooner severed the sheets of blubber from the underlying tissue and they were lifted by ropes that ran from the cradle, a kind of crow's nest on the mast. As the sheet was drawn up, two men pulled it in with hooks while two more cut it into pieces about one foot square and removed the adhering

7. A sperm whale in its death throes. The scene shows how the whalers had to deal with the stricken animal at dangerously close range. These crews are lucky to have their ship nearby. The whale making a fountain on the horizon suggests that the artist was not a whaler. (From *The Naturalist's Library* conducted by Sir William Jardine, Bart.)

8. Loading the harpoon gun. Note the wire loop through the shaft and the cords holding the flukes in place. The grenade has not been attached. When the harpoon is in place it is secured by cord to the two lugs on the top of the muzzle

9. Secured by a chain around the tail stock, a whale is towed alongside a catcher

10. A fin whale carcase is cast free with a marker flag, radar reflector and radio beacon. A killer whale porpoises behind it; the birds are cape pigeons, storm petrels and an albatross

flesh. These men were called krenders as they removed the flesh or 'kreng' which would cause the blubber to ferment if left on. The squares were dragged to the starboard side of the ship and laid, skin-side down, on a bench; when stripped off the skin the blubber was minced and pushed into a trough running behind the bench. The final task was to push the oily mess along the trough and down a canvas chute into the hold where it was packed into barrels. The cutting up and packing of the blubber was known as 'making-off', from the Dutch *afmaaken* – to finish or complete.

When the blubber has been stripped from one side of the carcase, the whalebone was cut out and the whale turned over so that the rest of the blubber could be removed. Finally, the body was cast off and allowed to float away.

As the decline of the Spitzbergen fishery set in after 1636 fewer ships brought home full cargoes, although at the end of the century the catch around Spitzbergen was still about 2,000 whales a year. By 1720, however, there were no more whales left in the area, Smeerenburg and the other factories fell into ruins and Spitzbergen became deserted except for occasional visits from explorers. The whalers had moved to new hunting grounds: along the ice edge to the east of Greenland, in Baffin Bay and up the Davis Strait. This new fishery started in 1719 when Dutch ships entered the Davis Straits. It flourished throughout the eighteenth century and continued into the twentieth century. When it started the Dutch were still supreme and the English whaling industry had begun a temporary decline.

To bolster an industry that brought in such essential materials as train-oil and whalebone, but suffered from the attacks of foreign privateers, the British Government introduced a bounty system, paying towards the cost of fitting out whaling-ships. In 1748 £1 was paid for each ton of the ship and this was doubled in 1750. In 1777 for instance, the *Volunteer* of Whitby received a bounty of £800, equal to one-ninth of the value of her cargo. She had caught five whales that yielded 65 tons of train-oil, worth £1,300, and 4–5 tons of whalebone, worth £2,300.

Throughout the seventeenth century wars had their effect on shipping. During the French wars and the American Revolution, English ships suffered from attacks by privateers and at the close of the century the Royal Navy had taken to escorting the whaling fleet to and from the Arctic. The Dutch fleet suffered at the hands of British and French navies and in 1798 a British convoying force captured the Dutch ships and never again was Holland a leader among whaling nations. The hunt for Greenland right whales in Arctic waters fell increasingly to the British and Americans, whose exploits and fortunes are described in Chapter 12.

10. The Sperm-Whalers

At the same time as the British whalers started their hunt for whales in Arctic waters, colonists in the New World began to harvest the rich crop of whales that travelled close to the shores of Newfoundland and New England. The beginnings of this whale-fishery are open to question. It seems certain that stranded whales offered the same bounty as they did on the other side of the Atlantic and that the proceeds were divided among those that had helped cut up and boil the blubber on an improvised tryworks on the shore, with a proportion going to the church.

It was only a short step from the dismembering of stranded whales to the harpooning and towing ashore of whales that appeared close to the land. The uncertainty lies in the manner by which the colonists became acquainted with whaling techniques. It has often been suggested that the English settlers copied the methods of the Indians, who certainly knew how to pursue whales at the time of the colonists' arrival. However, Edouard Stackpole, who has written a very thorough history of American whaling in *The Sea-Hunters*, contends that it was the Indians who took over European methods to improve on their primitive techniques of harassing and killing. The Europeans probably adapted some of the Indians' equipment, such as 'drogues' – balks of timber attached to the whale-line to brake the whale's escape, and they definitely employed Indians as look-outs and crewmen. Although it cannot be proved from documentary evidence that the European settlers brought their own methods of whale hunting it seems clear that this was so from the similarity of the whaling gear and techniques of the American whalers to those of the early Basques and contemporary European whalers working in Arctic waters.

The first whaling expeditions around the Nantucket coast, the birthplace of American whaling, and from the colonies at New York and Connecticut were quite simple. Small boats patrolled the shore, staying away from home for only a couple of weeks and dragging their whales ashore to try-out the blubber on the beach. The whales so caught were humpbacks and right whales, species that travel close to the shore on migration. The sperm whales, which were to become the main quarry for American whalers and on which their prosperity and reputation were founded, kept farther offshore and were not hunted until a whale-ship was accidentally blown out to sea in 1712, about a century after the start of the colonists' pursuit of whales.

The captain, Christopher Hussey, found himself among a school of sperm whales, killed one and towed it home. Sperm whale oil had already been obtained from stranded carcases and its excellence was appreciated, so the New Englanders readily followed Hussey's lead and set out after sperm whales on six-week cruises, bringing the blubber home in barrels. From this chance encounter the great sperm whale-fishery was set in being. It flourished until the early part of the nineteenth century, when whalers were scouring every corner of the oceans for their quarry, and lingered on for another century, until modern steam catchers equipped with heavy harpoon guns took over. It now survives in the Azores and other out of the way places where the whales are killed for local use.

Whaling developed rapidly on the New England coast and there was a boom in the latter half of the seventeenth century which extended into the eighteenth. From the island of Nantucket whaling spread to other harbours and ports, such as Martha's Vineyard, Salem, New Bedford and Sag Harbour. At the same time the Dutch colonists were hunting whales from New York and the French at Quebec were employing Basque harpooners. The oil and whalebone taken from the whales were in demand in the expanding colonies and also formed a very valuable source of revenue when exported to England, where an increasing population and developing industries demanded more oil for lighting and lubrication. Train-oil and whalebone from right whales, sperm-oil, and candles made from spermaceti, received high prices. Furthermore, the British Government granted concessions to the whaling industry. Bounties were given to whalers on each side of the Atlantic, as both the New England whalers and those sailing from British ports needed compensation from the depredations of foreign privateers who found the cumbersome whale-ships an easy and profitable prey.

The shore-fishery for whalebone whales gradually declined during the early part of the eighteenth century, but sperm-whaling on the high seas burgeoned as the whalers discovered new fishing grounds in both North and South Atlantic. The sperm whale lacked the valuable whalebone of the humpback and right whales but its blubber oil had valuable properties of its own and there was also the spermaceti from the head and the chance of striking lucky and finding ambergris.

In their early voyages the American whalers followed the example of their European counterparts in tearing the blubber off the whale as it lay alongside the ship and stowing it in barrels. Trying-out was conducted on land when the voyage was over but, as the ships stayed away from port for longer periods, it became necessary to treat the blubber immediately so that its bulk was reduced and spoilage was prevented. European whalers had been deterred from erecting tryworks on board after several ships had caught fire, and immediate trying-out was less important on their short voyages in cold climates. For the Americans with their long cruises in tropical waters the situation was different and they appear to have developed a practical shipborne tryworks without encountering any disasters.

The tryworks made a whaling vessel unmistakable. Sitting amidships, it appeared as a giant field-kitchen of brick, bound with iron braces; five feet high and about ten feet square, with two 200-gallon pots set over a primitive furnace. Whaling ships were blunt and broad in the beam – 'built by the mile and cut off in lengths as you want 'em' – and the square tryworks, stout spars and all the paraphernalia of dealing with gigantic whale carcases added to the impression of a floating factory, so different from the graceful, speedy clippers that quartered the same seas. For safety's sake the tryworks stood in a one-foot deep tray of water which prevented the deck from scorching and catching fire. Over the furnace there stood iron flues to prevent the oil slopping into the furnace as the ship rolled and pitched. Surrounding the tryworks were the accessories of trying-out: a machine to cut up the blubber, a wooden vessel to hold the raw slices and a copper tank in which the oil stood to cool before being stowed in barrels.

The cutting-in of a sperm whale was conducted along the same lines as with a right whale. The whale was securely fastened to the ship's side and a 'cutting-in stage' of stout planks rigged around it. A handrail helped to steady the officers as they attacked the carcase with long-handled 'spades' and ropes around their waists assured their safety. The first job was to cut off the head, severing it just behind the skull, a difficult job that involved careful dissection and manoeuvring of the huge weight of the whale.

First, a hole was cut in the blubber between one eye and one flipper. A large hook was inserted and the strain taken on the lifting tackle until the whale rolled on its side. A chain was passed around the lower jaw and raised, so that the whale rolled on to its back and the lower jaw could be cut off and lifted inboard. The whale was then turned on the other side, cuts made in the head, chains passed through the snout to secure it and one of the most difficult manoeuvres attempted. The chains holding the flukes and the body behind the eye were slacked off and the crew combined to haul in the tackle attached to the snout. This brought the whale into a vertical position, head uppermost, and the officers were able to cut around the base of the skull, the weight of the body assisting in tearing the flesh, until the neck bones were severed. The head was left to float astern until the blubber had been dealt with, and, presumably, the crew had paused to relax from the mental and physical strain.

A bald description of the removal of the head cannot convey the difficulties and dangers of the operation when a large sperm whale was being cut-in with a heavy sea running. The officers must have risked being swept off the stage, crushed by the whale or even severely gashed by their sharp tools at every turn, while the crew had to exert every sinew at the windlass to drag the carcase into position. According to accounts there were some whaling captains that did not allow their crews the luxury of a rest until the job of cutting-in was completely finished; not even allowing them to recover from the rigours of chasing the whale and towing it back to the ship before starting to cut-in. There was some necessity in this high-handed action as a whale could easily be lost if a storm blew up, so setting to naught the crew's earlier exertions.

After the head had been removed, the fluke chain was hauled tight again and the blubber stripped off in a spiral sheet, the body rolling over and over as the tackle attached to the blubber behind the eye was taken in. The sheet of blubber was cut into 'blanket pieces' as it came aboard and these were stowed in the 'blubber room' below decks. Attention now returned to the head which was lifted on board by the exertions of the whole crew, if it came from a small whale, or secured to the side of the ship, if too large to be brought on board. The head of the sperm whale is the repository of the spermaceti, which is liquid at body temperature but solidifies as it cools. The lower part of the head was called the 'junk' and contained spermaceti in a mass of tough, white fibres. The junk was cut off and put to one side for treatment later, while the upper part of the head – the 'case' – was opened to reveal a reservoir of pure spermaceti. This was baled out into casks and the remains of the head thrown overboard to complete the process of cutting-in.

Figure 13 Cutting-in a sperm whale. A–A removes the jaw, B–B removes the head and the blubber is cut off in a strip from A–A to C–C.

There remained one task before the carcase was set free to drift away. According to Murphy, the officers thrust sharp cutting spades deep into the whale's guts and, withdrawing them, carefully smelt the blades for any trace of ambergris. This evil-smelling lumpy substance was an occasional bonus for the sperm-whalers. At one time it was thought to come only from sick sperm whales but it has now been found in the intestines of healthy whales. After exposure to the air ambergris loses its offensive odour and, until the introduction of synthetics it was used, like musk and civet, as a base for perfumes. It fetched an extremely high price, once as high as £5 per ounce; in 1912 a whaling company was saved from liquidation by the discovery of a 1,000 lb lump of ambergris which was sold for £23,000.

Ambergris has been of value since the ninth century when pieces were found cast up on the shore. It was used in medicines, to spice wines, as an aphrodisiac, as well as a base for perfumes. Its origin was unknown until 1724 and, although it was once thought to be the equivalent of a pearl in an oyster – a special secretion for covering the sharp beaks of squids, its function is still a mystery.

Once free of the carcase, it was time for trying-out the blubber. The blanket pieces were brought up on deck and sliced into 'horse-pieces' either with a two-handed knife, or with a machine in which a knife rose and fell as a wheel was turned. The horse-pieces were not cut into slices like a side of bacon but only deeply scored, leaving the skin at the back intact to hold the thin strips of blubber like the leaves of a coarse, oily book. The slicing into horse-pieces allowed the oil to be rapidly cooked out of the blubber.

The harpooners were in charge of the trying-out, throwing horse-pieces into the large pots and ladling off the hot oil into a cooling tank. The process was extremely economical as the only fuel used was scrap or fritters, the crisp, brown tissue that is the remains of the horse-pieces after the oil has been removed. It burns with a hot, clean flame and, to sailors on other ships, the sight of a whaling vessel at work after nightfall must have presented an eerie sight as it drifted under a minimum of canvas with the wheel lashed down and the rigging, and toiling crew, lit up by the glare of the tryworks fire. To the crew of the whaler, trying-out was a messy business as the decks and their clothes became saturated with oil. The scuppers were blocked before cutting-in started so that the oil swilling over the deck could not escape. One of the last chores was to mop up this oil and add it to the rest in the trypots. When all the blubber had been disposed of, the decks and the men were thoroughly washed down and the barrels of oil taken below and securely stowed.

At the home port the oil was subjected to further processing. It was cleaned of dirt and left to stand for the winter to become a near solid 'black cake', which was squeezed in a press to produce 'winter-oil'. This would not freeze in the winter. Second and third pressings gave lower quality 'spring-' and 'summer-oil'. The residue was used in the manufacture of candles. The fine spermaceti wax was used in cosmetics and medicines.

During their toils among the heaps of blubber the whaling crew could content themselves with the thought that each barrel filled brought their home-coming nearer and brought more money into their pockets. Throughout the eighteenth century the New England sperm-whalers prospered. The price of sperm-oil had risen to £40 a ton by 1770 and in that year, Nantucket alone had a fleet of over a hundred ships, whose catch was valued at £150,000. But five years later the American whaling industry was hit by the first of several disasters.

The British Government, which had once supported the American whalers with bounties, now started to act against them. In 1766 a duty was placed on oil and whalebone imported from America, while bounties were still given to whalers sailing from Great Britain. Yet when the Americans' dissatisfaction with the British Government boiled over into the War of Independence the whaling ports were still closely bound to the home country. Nantucket became a haven for loyalists and the whalers were caught in a crossfire. The revolutionaries on the mainland refused to trade with the people on the island of Nantucket and British privateers waited to snap up any ships that came their way and forced their crews to serve as British seamen.

By diplomacy and cunning, the Nantucketers attempted to continue their trade in whales throughout the war, but by the end only thirty-five whaling ships remained of the one hundred and thirty-two that existed in 1775. Rebel ports suffered worse: in retaliation for the activities of their privateers, New Bedford and other villages were attacked and looted by the British and their ships were destroyed. After the war, the Nantucketers found the British market still closed by a formidable tariff wall and attempts were made to trade with the French.

Despite these political troubles the whaling industry flourished and the whalers pushed farther across the oceans in search of their quarry. At first they sailed to the Caribbean Sea and the Gulf of Mexico. The 'Brazil Banks' fishery started in 1744 and in 1765 American whalers were crossing the Atlantic to the Western Islands, as they called the Azores, and to the coast of Africa. A rich fishing ground was also found around the Falkland Islands and the River Plate, but the real breakthrough was the discovery in mid nineteenth century, of whaling grounds in the Indian and Pacific Oceans. This led to the peak of American sperm-whaling and the four- or five-year voyages experienced by Melville and Bullen.

Ironically the two main discoveries in the Pacific were made by British ships, although one at least was manned by Nantucketers who had moved to England after the War of Independence. In 1788 the *Emelia*, belonging to the Enderby brothers, whose company combined exploration with whaling, sailed around Cape Horn into the Pacific and hunted in what later became known as the Chile Coast or 'On-shore' fishing grounds. In 1819, another

Figure 14 The main sperm-whaling grounds of the world.

Charleston

Gulf of Mexico

Bahama

Caribbean

Azores or
Western
Isles

Canary

Cape Verde

Coast of Africa

Brazil
Banks

Ascension

St. Helena

Carroll
Ground

Walvis Bay

Cape Town

Tristan da Cunha

Falkland Islands

South Georgia

British ship, the Syren, started the exploitation of the 'Coast of Japan' as the north-west Pacific was called by whalemen.

Fishing in the last of the major sperm-whaling grounds to be discovered was known as 'cruising down the line', a phrase that referred to sailing the seas bordering the equator. In theory a Pacific cruise was idyllic, with the tropical sun beating down and palm-laden Pacific Islands, such as Hawaii and the Fijis, to visit, but in practice it was probably as unpleasant as buffeting through the stormy seas of higher latitudes. The sun's heat boiled the pitch that caulked the deck timbers, making the crowded, airless fo'c'sle a Black Hole. Visits to Pacific islands usually meant hard work in filling water casks and cutting firewood. Even the chance of going ashore to get roaring drunk might be spoiled by unfriendly natives who made it necessary to fight off fleets of canoes with harpoon and lance.

The rigours and questionable delights of these long voyages, tedious, although not monotonous, and broken only by the danger of storms and whale-catching, have been preserved in several books written by the men who took part. Some are a disappointment to anyone wishing to learn more about whaling. The author has often assumed that his readers are familiar with the techniques of sailing as well as whaling and becomes expansive only when dealing with topics unrelated to whaling, such as a visit to an island or a fight amongst the crew. For instance, Nelson Cole Haley, who ran away from home to go a-whaling, assumes his readers are sailors and describes two ships meeting for a 'gam' in *Whale Hunt*:

> Standing along until the other ship bore about two points forward of our lee beam, our wheel was put hard up and the yards squared. As the ship got before the wind and pointed her flying jibboom for the mainmast, he at the same time hauled aback his main-topsail, and being not far apart, we soon came within speaking distance.

Without a knowledge of sailing this is meaningless but it describes a ticklish manoeuvre in which one ship headed straight for the other then, just as collision seemed inevitable, swung away to pass behind the other's stern, so close that the captains could exchange news in normal voices.

Frank Bullen, on the other hand, who was once a London street-arab and who went whaling more by mistake than intention, is at pains to describe the technicalities of life on a whale-ship, and so his narrative comes to life and the reader can readily visualize the scenes and activities. A further difference between *Whale Hunt* and Bullen's *Cruise of the Cachalot* is that Bullen, who had had experience on merchant ships, was sympathetic towards the greenhorns in the whaling crew, whereas Haley, the professional, is scathing about their shortcomings. It was usual for a whale-ship to carry in its crew inexperienced members who were either city riffraff or country lads from landbound states. To them, the sea itself was a novelty, let alone the experiences of climbing along the yards many feet above a bucking deck to reef a sail or rowing a frail boat right up to a thrashing sperm whale. One can easily imagine the terror of the seasick men as they attempted to carry out incomprehensible but forcefully expressed orders. The saying that a soldier has to fear his officers more than the enemy must also have applied to whalers.

The raw crews received their shakedown on crossing the Atlantic from New England to the Azores. They were assigned to watches for working the ship and to crews for the boats while the experienced men broke out the whaling gear, fitted out the boats, and masthead look-outs swept the sea for tell-tale spouts, crying 'She blows' to rouse the crew and send the captain leaping up the rigging.

In parenthesis, it should be noted here that the chroniclers of American sperm-whaling often differ in their descriptions and occasionally criticize each other openly. It has been pointed out that Herman Melville's 'There she blows!' is too longwinded a cry for an excited look-out. He was more likely to sing out 'She blows!', 'Ah blows!' or just 'Blows!' and it is interesting that the present-day Azores whalers, who use the equipment and techniques of the American sperm-whalers, sing our '*bloz!*'. More importantly, William Williams of *One Whaling Family*, points out that Melville's exciting description of the boats being rowed after the whale with the officers bellowing exhortation 'just never happened'. The whole art of 'going on' a whale consisted of sneaking up without it being frightened or 'gallied'. To this end, the boats sailed to within a hundred yards of the whale, then a change was made to paddling. Lowering the sail and mast, or shipping the oars, was a ticklish task that had to be accomplished without knocking the hull of the boat and alerting the whale. Whalers only rowed on to a whale when it was about to sound and speed was the prime consideration.

However, to take one step back, after a whale was sighted the boats were swung out in readiness for the order to lower away as the ship closed with its quarry. The typical American whaling boat was an excellent sea-boat, pointed at each end, 20–30 feet long and six feet in beam. Until the middle of the nineteenth century, whale-boats were clinker-built with overlapping planks; but carvel-built boats with flush planking became popular, as they ran through the water with less noise. In the bow there was a groove through which the line ran, held in place by a pin. Three feet back was the 'clumsy-cleat' or 'thighboard', a thwart with a notch in which the harpooner braced his leg to steady himself. In the middle of the boat were five thwarts for the oarsmen then another clumsy-cleat for the steersman who worked the long steering oar, and the loggerhead, an eight-inch post around which the line ran. A surprising amount of gear fitted into the boat: six harpoons, three lances, mast, sails, two tubs with 1,800 feet of line, a drogue for slowing down a running whale, hatchet, bailer, boathook and grapnel for securing the dead whale, keg with lantern, matches and emergency food, and so on.

As the boats set after the whale, two harpoons were attached to the line and rested in a crotch for immediate use. The officer in charge stood in the stern and guided his boat on to the whale. In this he was assisted from the ship, which was manned by a skeleton crew who gave signals in the form of flags hoisted or sails rearranged. For instance 'Whales ahead of ship' was signalled by lowering the flying jib and 'Whales between the boats' by raising flags at the fore and main mastheads.

To approach within harpooning distance, about 16–18 feet, the officer had to approach head-on – 'going on head and head' – or from behind – 'going on the flukes' – so that the whale did not see him. At the crucial moment, he pushed on the long steering oar to swing bow-on to the whale, the harpoon was darted, and a quick backstroke with the paddles lifted the boat clear.

The harpooner had little time to take aim and dart, but the harpoon had to go behind the head to avoid the skull and, for preference, it had to enter the arched back. If the back were depressed when the harpoon struck it was likely to be thrown out when the back arched and the wound enlarged. William

Scoresby tells of a harpoon that was thrown clear into the air as the whale arched its back, but landed again point first and struck firmly into the whale which, in due course, was captured.

To hold firm, the harpoon had to penetrate the blubber, leaving its wooden pole behind, and fasten firmly in the underlying muscles. It was not unusual for a poorly thrown harpoon to draw and often a second was thrown for extra security immediately after the first. An improved harpoon, the toggle-iron, was invented by James Temple, a negro blacksmith of New Bedford, in 1848. The single barb was mounted on a pivot and held closed by a stub of wood, which shattered as it entered the whale and allowed the barb to swing out.

Figure 15 Toggle-iron harpoon (a), showing the movement of the barb, and (b) hand lance (modified from Scammon).

The whale's reaction to harpooning was usually to sound, taking 600–1,200 feet of line, then to charge off at the surface. As the line sang out it was essential to see that no kinks or loops appeared that could whip a man overboard or tear off a limb. Yet at this stage a most alarming manoeuvre took place. The officer, known as the boatheader, left his steering oar and swapped places with the harpooner or boatsteerer, hopping from thwart to thwart. Melville considered this a foolish and needless custom, yet Professor Dakin found that it had persisted when he visited Twofold Bay, Australia in 1932 just as this relic of the old sperm-whaling day was about to close. As far as he could gather the swap-over was carried out because one man was a specialist with the harpoon and the other knew how to use a lance. Apparently one man could not be expected to do both. However, Azores whalers of the present-day, who learned whaling from the Americans, do not bother to change places in the boat, neither did the British whalers.

If the greenhorns were lucky they were able to practise these manoeuvres on pilot whales or blackfish. The body blubber from these small cetaceans was hardly worth collecting but that from the head, particularly from the melon, was thirty times more valuable. Each animal gave about five gallons of very fine oil which was used as a lubricant in watches and other delicate machinery, and at one time the flesh was salted or dried and traded for fresh food in Dominica. After experience with blackfish, the greenhorns might not be so stricken with terror on meeting a sperm whale, but it was often necessary for the officer to keep a close check on his crew to prevent them jumping overboard, to everybody's jeopardy, and if there were ever a series of accidents the crews sometimes became too scared to even man the boats.

After the whale had been harpooned and had set off on its blind chase, things became more orderly for the moment. The whale-boat was towed willy-nilly through the waves in what was known as a Nantucket sleigh ride. The crew, meanwhile, exerted themselves to pull in the straining line until the bow was near enough – 'wood to blackskin' – for the boatheader to thrust in his lance (Figure 15a). If the boat could not be brought sufficiently near for this, the boatheader might try 'pitch-poling' – tossing the lance like a caber and drawing it back on a line. He could also try to slow a strong whale by 'spading the flukes' – cutting at the small of the tail with a boat-spade, an instrument like a giant chisel with a six-foot handle. Spading cut the tendons linking the flukes with the propulsive muscles – throwing the whale out of gear, as it were – and severed large veins so the whale bled to death.

At last the whale would go into its death throes or flurry, heralded by its spouting blood – 'It's chimney's on fire' was the cry as the boat's crew were drenched in a fine red mist. Then the gigantic animal would thrash in circles, rearing its head and crashing its tail down until it finally rolled on its side in a welter of foam – 'fin out'.

11. A whale-catcher steams past the hills of South Georgia. Note the high, flared bows, the catwalk running from the bridge and the crow's nest

12. The factory at Grytviken. A whale is being dismembered on the plan and another floats offshore

13. Japanese flensers make the first cuts in a fin whale with long-handled knives. The catcher behind them has its gun loaded

14. The plan at Hvalfordur, Iceland, showing a sei whale stripped of its blubber, which lies in strips to the left. The steam saw for cutting up bones is on the right

11. The Decline of the Sperm-Whalers

In the heyday of sperm-whaling the grounds were often so crowded with whale-ships that their crews had to compete for the whales. Boats from two or more ships might chase one whale, the prize going to the crew that first got its harpoons in, but if these pulled out the whale was once more fair game for anyone. Sometimes two ships 'mated', cruising together, but well spaced to increase the area covered by the look-outs, and co-operating in the killing of whales. The accounts of whaling in this period give the impression that the Americans had a monopoly of sperm-whaling, but in fact other nations also participated. Nevertheless the Americans were the most successful, as shown by one instance in which boats from the United States, England, France and Portugal chased the same whale during a flat calm. The Americans got the first harpoon in because, it was said, it was the habit of American boatheaders to use one hand to push the oar of the stroke oarsman while working the steering oar with the other.

The peak of the New England whaling came in 1846, at a time when whalers were sending barrels of oil home by merchant ships before returning fully laden themselves, but before the peak period the industry had weathered one more crisis: the second destruction of the whaling fleet by the British Navy. Prior to this there had been an undeclared war with France in which more ships than ever were lost to privateers. Then in 1812 a war broke out between Americans and Canadians, the latter comprising French, British and Red Indians. Apart from the campaigns on land, the Royal Navy blockaded Nantucket and other whaling ports. News of the war was slow in reaching the ships, nearly all of which were cruising the Pacific whaling grounds, and they were captured, sometimes within sight of home, as they returned laden with oil from their long voyages. The population of Nantucket suffered severe privations during the blockade; but such was the demand for whale products that soon after peace came in 1815 the industry was back in full swing. The Pacific 'off-shore' grounds and the Coast of Japan were opened up and exploited, while three species of whalebone whale, the bowhead or Greenland right whale, the humpback and the gray whale, were the objects of pursuit, leading the whalers down the coast of California and up through the Bering Straits.

The sperm whale boom did not last long for the New England ports and during the second half of the nineteenth century the industry slowly declined. The fall was not due to any one factor and the importance of any one cause is obscured by the influence of others. It is very likely that the stocks of sperm whales were being over-exploited, although this did not have an immediate effect because whalebone whales were taken in larger numbers. The introduction of kerosene made from mineral oil for lighting in 1859 removed one of the main outlets for sperm-oil; but its introduction was gradual, and there was still a demand for sperm-oil in the fast-growing industries of the nineteenth century. It was, for instance, still burnt in lighthouses and railway signalling lamps.

During the American Civil War the New England whaling fleet was destroyed for the third and last time. Once again the whalers were unaware that a war was in progress and they were captured by Southern privateers as they sailed up the Atlantic. Later, the steam ship *Shenandoah* entered the Pacific to ravage Unionist shipping there and captured and burned thirty whale-ships. Eventually owners kept their ships lying idle in port for safety, or sold them. Then, finally, in 1861, forty whale-ships were gathered in New Bedford harbour and loaded with rocks. They set sail on November 16th as the 'Stone fleet' and were sunk at the entrance of Charleston harbour to foil privateers and blockade runners.

New England whalers were unable to recover from this disaster as they had from previous destructions, and the cause probably lies in the removal of the focal point of the whaling industry across the continent to San Francisco and, to a lesser extent, Honolulu. As most sperm whales were taken in the Pacific it was an obvious step to base the whaling fleet there, so cutting out the time-consuming journeys up and down the length of the Atlantic and around the dangerous Capes of Horn and Good Hope. The opening-up of the American West provided a nearby market and a bridgehead for export of oil to the rest of North America. San Francisco became the new centre of whaling but this is not how the city is remembered. In 1849 the California gold-rush started, and although the owners of whaling-ships were provided with a new market they had also to contend with vanishing crews who deserted in search of easier ways of getting rich.

A lust for gold was not necessary to drive a man to desert his ship. Apart from the professional 'career' whalers who hoped to become harpooners, officers and eventually gain the command of their own ships, and the men shipped from the Azores, Cape Verdes or Pacific Islands, the crew of a whaling-ship during the nineteenth century were unlikely to have entered this profession from choice.

Some whalers were seamen with such a poor reputation that no merchant ship would take them, which means that they must have been at the rock-bottom of the social strata; others signed on because no other employment seemed forthcoming and debts were piling up. The keepers of low dockside lodgings would allow bills to run up then recouped their losses, together with a commission, by supplying their erstwhile lodgers to a whaling-ship. Protest was kept to a minimum by ensuring that the draftees were soundly drunk. By the time they came round, it was too late – the ship was at sea and the officers had the upper hand. Other men might find themselves being tricked into sailing on a whale-ship. Like Bullen, they might sign the ship's articles without knowing what sort of ship it was. They were then allowed to settle debts and collect their belongings under escort, and taken out to the ship where it was riding at anchor to make escape impossible.

To keep this sort of crew in order needed strong discipline – commonly at the end of an officer's arm, but force was probably fairly administered for most of the time. Whaling officers worked their way up from the fo'c'sle, so they had to undergo a process of natural selection: only the fittest, capable of dominating subordinates, survived to make the quarterdeck. Under such a regime a voyage might be bearable, provided that good whaling provided plenty of hard work and prospects of a quick return home, but a bullying officer, a failure to catch whales and a few mishaps made escape from the ship very desirable. San Francisco and the goldfields, or the Pacific islands with their promise of an idle life in a permissive society were strong temptations.

Melville, the arch-romantic of whaling, deserted his ship in the Marquesas and it was reckoned that few American whalers returned home in the same ship as they had set sail.

Added to the natural dangers of whaling and a tough discipline, there was the poor food, supplemented only by such fish as could be caught and fresh fruit bought at stopping places, and living space was confined to cramped, murky quarters in the fo'c'sle. Yet in song and writing sperm-whaling has become a romance, that is an adventure and excitement. The hard, dangerous, yet everyday work of the whale crews would now be thought of as adventure and worthy of the publicity given to the climbing of mountains or sailing of small boats by men whose thirst for physical excitement and achievement can no longer be satisfied by a regular job.

Out of the routine of trimming sails and working up whales there stand some episodes that show up sperm-whaling as an exciting and adventurous occupation. Such stories fire the imagination; they may cause a sense of loss that such things no longer happen, and 'running away to sea' is no longer worth the dreams of an adventurous boy. Yet when they happened they could not have been fun or exciting, merely terrifying and agonizing. It is a strange quirk of human nature that the stories of boldly facing up to danger that lead men to joining risky operations, whether military, professional or exploratory, are of just those incidents which are better avoided by anyone who values his life.

One such story is that of the disaster that befell the American North Pacific whaling fleet when beset by ice and is described in the next chapter. The fate of the Nantucket ship *Essex* is yet more incredible and although it was a disaster on a smaller scale, the suffering was infinitely greater. In November 1820, the *Essex* was working near the equator, midway between the Marquesas and the Galapagos. While chasing sperm whales, the boat belonging to Owen Chase, the mate, was struck by a whale and had to set back to the ship. Not long after, Chase saw a large sperm whale near the ship. It immediately turned towards the ship and rammed it at full speed. The shock jarred the ship, leaving it quivering and leaking badly, but, as soon as the pumps had been rigged, the whale struck again and stove in the bows.

This was not the first time that a ship had been struck by a sperm whale and in this case the first collision was probably accidental while the second may have been inspired by rage. The question of the whale's motive was academic to the men on the *Essex*, as she settled rapidly. Grabbing some navigational equipment, they jumped into the damaged whale-boat and drew away to await the return of the other two boats. The captain was the first to draw near. The poor man was shattered by the sudden and apparently inexplicable wreck of his ship. ' "My God, Mr Chase, what is the matter?" I [Chase] answered, "We have been stove by a whale" ' – a succinct dialogue as memorable as 'Dr Livingstone, I presume'.

The *Essex* had not completely disappeared and the men were able to retrieve a small quantity of food and gear before they set sail for the American mainland, so avoiding the Marquesas, which they believed to be inhabited by cannibals, and the Sandwich Islands, where a hurricane season was thought to be in progress. Nearly four weeks later they sighted land, the small and almost barren, Henderson's Island. After a week they set off again, leaving three men there, and their suffering took a new and grisly turn. Racked by hunger and thirst, as well as by their desperate situation, three of the crew died. But, in doing so, they saved their companions, who forced themselves to eat their flesh.

Chase's boat became separated from the others and was picked up by a ship after covering 3,700 miles. The other two boats had a worse fate. One disappeared without trace and in the captain's boat the survivors ran out of food. There was only one thing to do. Lots were cast, and Owen Coffin, the captain's nephew, lost. He was killed and eaten. Three weeks later, three months after leaving the *Essex*, the survivors were picked up. Of the nine men that survived the wreck of the *Essex*, all went back to sea and all eventually gained command of ships.

The story of the *Essex* must be one of the grimmest episodes in the history of whaling, but lesser disasters were frequent as the men battled with their giant quarry. Strokes from the lashing flukes caused death or ghastly wounds and the harpoon line accounted for injuries ranging from burns to death by drowning as it was swept out of the boat by the whale. Scammon tells of an officer, nicknamed 'Jabe', who was entangled in a line and only saved by the harpoon drawing out, and Svend Føyn suffered a similar accident. Scammon also records the accidents that befell the crew of one ship in the course of one day's whaling. The whale struck one boat, breaking the leg of one man and the arm of another, together with minor injuries to others. A second boat, coming to help was also struck causing injuries to many of the crew. All were eventually rescued but half the ship's company had been injured and most of the rest badly frightened. Two boats were launched a few days later but the crews jumped overboard as soon as they neared a whale. However, even this panic-stricken action could have its amusing side as when a notorious braggart leaped headlong over the side of his boat and landed on the whale's back. The whale slowly submerged leaving the man floundering.

The decline of the sperm-whalers was gradual and almost painless. The use of kerosene developed gradually so that the demand for sperm-oil fell only slowly. Whalebone from bowheads, humpbacks and gray whales was still in demand and made whaling voyages profitable. So there was no sudden laying-up of ships and no unemployment.

Whale-ships continued to sail out of New England and Pacific ports but in ever decreasing numbers, until World War I when U-boat warfare created a shortage of oils and fats and demand for whale-oil rose again. In 1918 there was an attempt in the United States to introduce whalemeat for human consumption. The meat was cut up, cooled, soaked in brine to remove blood and the strong taste, then tinned. The experiment was not a success and the old-time Yankee sperm-whalers eventually died out, the end coming in 1925 when the *John R Manta* and the *Margarett* returned to New Bedford from their last cruises.

The Americans had, however, left a legacy in the form of open-boat whaling in other parts of the world.

In the early part of the nineteenth century there had been a considerable sperm whale-fishery around the coasts of Australia and New Zealand. Later the colonists there took up the chase and developed a flourishing industry for both sperm whales and humpbacks. This continued as a relic industry at Twofold Bay in New South Wales until 1932, by which time modern whaling with steam catchers had commenced. At the turn of the century one shore station in New Zealand employed strong nets for catching humpbacks. The whales became entangled as they swam close inshore and were lanced from boats. This technique was taken to Tonga where it is still practised.

Open-boat whaling using equipment identical to that used by American sperm-whalers had survived in two parts of the North Atlantic: in the West Indies and the Azores. The American whale-ships called at both groups of islands to pick up native boatmen as crew, and they developed the local whaling industries on their return.

In the West Indies, whaling is still carried on at St Vincent, St Lucia and Dominica. The catch once included humpbacks and sperm whales but now it is the smaller cetaceans, such as pilot whales, which are the main catch. Despite the introduction of outboard motors and shotguns to hurl the harpoon fifty yards, much farther than is possible by throwing, this little industry which may account for several hundred whales and porpoises in a year is probably doomed to wither as the tourist trade blossoms and provides easier ways of making a living. As a comment on the role of romance and excitement in whaling, it is recorded that one West Indian skipper gave it as his ambition to leave his boat and get a job in North America as a petrol station attendant.

The sperm-whaling industry based in the Azores is better known and is still flourishing with the addition of motor boats to tow the whale-boats close to the whale and to tow the carcase back, and radio sets for the lookouts to guide the whalers to their target. A detailed study of the techniques still in use has been made by Robert Clarke, who found that few innovations have been added to the old techniques. As already mentioned, the boatheader and boatsteerer do not change ends and the boat is longer than the American original and carries one more oarsman, otherwise the whalers of the Azores and West Indies are a living relic of by-gone days. Until recently most of the whales caught around the Azores were still tryed-out in iron pots on the shore, as they had been in seventeenth century New England and Spitzbergen.

12. Bowheads and Gray Whales

As the number of sperm whales caught began to drop during the nineteenth century more whalers turned to the Arctic regions of the Atlantic, where European whalers had been fishing sporadically since the seventeenth century for Greenland right whales or bowheads. Some time later, the American Pacific fleet entered the Sea of Okhotsk, the Bering Sea and finally penetrated the Bering Straits into the Arctic Ocean. The right whales were not such a dangerous quarry as sperm whales, but working in northern seas brought the constant danger of being trapped by ice. Many ships were lost, sometimes whole fleets at a time, but their crews usually escaped to other ships or reached land where they were sheltered by Eskimos.

Unlike the sperm whalers the right whale hunters were limited to short summer cruises, when the seas were relatively free from ice. British whalers left their home ports, such as Hull, Whitby and Dundee, in early March and called at Lerwick in the Shetland Islands to replenish their stores and sign on local men to complete their crews. As soon as the ship was sailing steadily northwards the boats' crews were chosen in a way that ensured a fair distribution and no favour. The crew lined up in rows and the harpooners gave their pocket knives to a boy who had never been to sea before. He laid one knife, not knowing to whom it belonged, in front of each row of men and they became the crew of the knife's owner. The crews then set to preparing the whaling gear, sharpening harpoons and lances and coiling the whale lines so that they were free of kinks.

During this period, at least, the whale-ship's crew were full of hope for success in what was one of the most speculative of occupations during this period. A successful season would result in a full pocket on the return home but it was not unknown for a ship to come home empty. This meant poverty for the crew, as they were paid starvation wages, any profit coming in the form of bonuses or bounties. At one time harpooners received only bounties, but in 1850 they received thirty shillings per month which was supplemented by bounties at the rate of twenty shillings per ton of whalebone, eight shillings per ton of oil and eight shillings for each whale harpooned. Mates were paid fifty-five shillings a month with proportionately larger bounties; but, as the crew had to buy their own tea, coffee, tobacco and other luxuries, they could come home from an unsuccessful cruise actually in debt. Those with families had to join coal ships for the winter, a blow to their pride as well as the loss of a well-earned rest.

When whales were scarce the whalers attempted to cut their losses by hunting seals, walruses and polar bears, particularly when heavy ice made whale-hunting impossible. Polar bears were also an additional prize when they gathered to feed off a whale carcase. They were usually shot and skinned but young ones were sometimes caught alive for zoos. A fine bear was worth £35, a good price in those days, but even a young polar bear needs to be treated with care. The best way of catching a bear was to throw a lasso over its neck as it was swimming, pulling in the slack rope until the bear was hard against the side of the boat. There is a story of one harpooner who neglected to secure the rope properly. The bear jumped aboard and the frightened crew scurried aft, leaving their weapons in the bows, but luckily the bear was just as scared and jumped out again.

A far less hazardous pastime was the killing of seals. Harp seals bear their young in March and the whaling ships called at the breeding grounds on the ice on their way north. Both adults and pups were killed, by clubbing or rifle fire, and their bodies carried on board for the skins to be removed and salted, while the blubber was packed in barrels. If a ship found a large concentration of pups its crew could dispose of 2,500 in a day, hard work when the pups were in peak condition and dangerous, too, if the ice were broken and a swell was running.

Even such a vast slaughter of seals was no more than a sideline to the serious business of whale catching. The boom in right-whaling in Arctic waters started in the second decade of the nineteenth century and between 1814 and 1817 there were nearly a hundred and fifty British ships working there each year. Up to this time most whalers had worked in the Greenland Sea, to the north of Iceland, with only a few sailing round the southern tip of Greenland into the Davis Strait. These grounds were poor but in 1817 two ships got past Disko Island into Baffin Bay (see Figure 17, p. 128) where they found whales to be plentiful. In the following years the Greenland Sea was virtually abandoned by all except Scandinavian sealers in favour of the rich hunting grounds on the east and west coasts of Baffin Bay.

The ships that sailed into the ice-infested waters west of Greenland had of necessity to be more strongly built than the ships engaged in sperm-whaling, and no right whaler suffered the fate of the *Essex*. However, their equipment was much the same, except that the look-out nestled in a barrel-like crow's nest rather than hanging on to an iron loop, and the blubber was stored in iron tanks without being tried-out. An important development in the early nineteenth century was the introduction of various types of harpoon guns. These were small compared with Svend Føyn's modern guns and were often hand-held.

Several attempts had been made to find ways of propelling a harpoon farther than could be effected by a man's strength. Harpoon guns were first tried out in the eighteenth century but they were not adopted because of reluctance to give up old, well-tried methods; a reluctance reinforced by accidents and the loss of whales through inexperience. Nevertheless, in 1772 the Society of Arts tried to popularize an improved version of its own guns by offering £1 for the best account of taking whales with it. This gun could hurl a harpoon forty yards, a great improvement over the range of the hand harpoon. Like modern harpoons, this harpoon had a slip-ring on the shaft that slid back to the butt and allowed the whaleline to steady the harpoon's flight.

By the 1850's most British ships carried harpoon guns that were mounted on swivels in the boats' bows. The Americans took longer to adopt them but during the second half of the century both nationalities hunted right whales with a strange assortment of firearms. The basic harpoon gun was Greener's gun. It had a three-foot barrel, a bore of $1\frac{1}{2}$ inches and fired a $4\frac{1}{2}$-foot harpoon about eighty yards with reasonable accuracy. After 1858 a new device began to supersede the hand lance. This was the bomb-lance which was fired either from the same Greener's gun as the harpoon or from a separate firearm. The bomb-lance consisted of a metal tube about twenty-one inches long with a sharp tip. As it left the gun elastic feathers unrolled from the tube to steady its flight, and a fuse was lit as the gun went off to detonate the powder charge after the bomb-lance had penetrated the whale.

With these two weapons whales could be killed without the boat having come within twenty-five yards and the dangers of the enterprise were considerably reduced. A third weapon was a combined hand harpoon and bomb-lance that dispensed with the dangers of using firearms in a small boat. It was an ingenious mechanism known by the cumbersome name of Pierce's harpoon-bomb-lance-gun. To the tip of a conventional harpoon shaft was

Figure 16 Pierce's harpoon-bomb-lance-gun (modified from Scammon).

attached the lock and one-foot barrel of the gun. A toggle-iron harpoon was clamped to the muzzle end of the barrel which was loaded with a sixteen-inch bomb-lance. The contrivance was darted at the whale by hand so that the harpoon made fast. As it entered the whale the trigger rod was pushed back tripping the firing mechanism and shooting the bomb-lance deep into the whale's body where it was detonated by a time fuse. The harpoon and its attached line came free so that the shaft and the precious gun could be hauled back to the boat on a thin line, while the harpoon was still fast.

Even with the help of explosives, right whales might take over twenty hours to kill, leaving the boat crew tired and frozen from the effort. Perhaps these were of the least of their worries because the Davis Strait and Baffin Bay were notorious for their ice. As well as icebergs there was heavy pack ice, thick floes that drifted down from the Arctic Ocean. If the whalers were lucky the ice broke up early in the spring and drifted southwards leaving open water. If not, they had to weave their way up leads of open water that might close at any moment, trapping the ship and perhaps crushing it. In this part of the world gales suddenly spring up, forcing the floes together so that they ride over each other, and icebergs drive through the pack crushing everything in their way. Even in a flat calm, when the surface of the sea is like a mirror, the pack ice may eerily creep forward, driven by currents or distant gales.

Against these overwhelming forces the whalers had to rely chiefly on their luck, but experience and expertise could help to alleviate the dangers. As far as was possible, the ships hugged the coastline. For one thing this was the place to find the whales, but if the ships could keep close inshore they avoided the largest floes and icebergs which grounded on the bottom off-shore. The disadvantages of this practice were the risk of running on to rocks in the uncharted waters and the danger of onshore winds driving them aground.

If a ship was caught by pack ice in the open sea one chance of avoiding being crushed was to saw docks in a large floe. Using sixteen-foot saws mounted on rockers and operated by sixteen men, a large chunk of ice could be cut out and floated away to form a deep slot in the floe. The ship was worked into the slot and moored with sea anchors. Here it was safe from the pressure of the ice outside, unless the floe forming the dock split up. If the floes did grip the ship, the crew's hope of salvation lay in the ice sliding under the keel to lift up the ship; because if the ship was nipped on the waterline the floes might splinter her timbers. Pressure from ice was alleviated by use of saws and explosive charges and the ship could sometimes be freed by shattering the ice with artificial waves: a stout rope was run from masthead to the ice and the crew hauled rhythmically, rolling the ship to shatter the ice around the hull.

Whaling ships were all too often caught by ice near the end of the season. Unless a gale broke the ice and blew it away they were then in danger of being trapped for the winter. The crews had to prepare for the worst by moving stores on to land, if there was any nearby, and by hunting for seals or fishing. Sometimes there would be other ships nearby that were clear of ice and half the men of the trapped ship would attempt to reach them by dragging their boats over the ice to open water. This hazardous undertaking was necessary because the ships did not carry enough supplies to feed the whole crew throughout an Arctic winter. This lack of foresight, or rather meanness, on the part of the ships' owners was to have disastrous consequences.

It had become the habit of the whalers to leave the relatively open waters of the west coast of Greenland and sail across Baffin Bay to Baffin Island where they would go 'rock nosing' – threading their way through the deep bays where whales abounded. There was a particular danger of being trapped by ice floes piling across the entrance of the bay and disaster came in 1830 when severe weather destroyed nineteen out of the ninety-one British ships that entered the Davis Strait. Hardly a whale was caught, and some whaling companies were put out of business. The remainder continued as before and in 1835 six more ships were lost and a further eleven were stuck in the ice for the winter. Although five were freed in the spring their crews suffered horribly. Weakened by shortage of food, they succumbed easily to frostbite and scurvy. Out of 600 men in the fleet one-fifth perished.

The incredible sequel to the disaster of 1835 is that the shipowners completely ignored its lessons and sent their ships back to the Davis Strait in 1836, still without adequate provisions for an enforced stay. Once again the ice closed in and six ships were trapped for the winter with all the ensuing suffering. It was only then that remedies were debated. Some ships began to carry the new invention of tinned food and the idea of wintering at a permanent base to cut out the dangerous journeys in and out of the Davis Strait was considered. One of the chief protagonists of wintering in the Arctic was Captain (later Sir) James Clark Ross, the famous explorer, who had been sent to the whalers' aid in HMS *Cove* in 1835.

The idea of spending winter at land stations was nearly as old as Arctic whaling itself. The first attempt was made by the English during the days of whaling at Spitzbergen. Volunteers to spend a winter at the whaling station at Spitzbergen were sought but none came forward, so a handful of condemned criminals were offered a free pardon if they would spend the winter there. Overjoyed, they were conveyed north but after one look at the grim, desolate scenery, they expressed preference for a quick death. They were, in fact, pardoned; but their misgivings about Spitzbergen were justified, for Dutch parties left for the winter were wiped out by scurvy. That Europeans could survive an Arctic winter was proved by accident when a group of

English whalers were marooned at a shore station. They survived a terrible winter by hunting and chewing the fritters left over from the summer's blubber boiling.

Ross' suggestions for a permanent base were taken up by William Penny, who later became famous for his expeditions in search of Sir John Franklin after he had failed to return from an attempt to find the North-west Passage. It was through Penny that whalers penetrated Cumberland Sound where a flourishing fishery later developed. Increasing numbers of whalers, particularly Americans, took to wintering in ships or on the shore. They went out on sorties from their bases in early spring to hunt whales amongst the floes, dragging the blubber and whalebone back over the ice. The Cumberland Sound fishery flourished until the 1860's when the Americans opened up Hudson's Bay but shore stations continued there until the 1930's.

The whalers could heave a sigh of relief as they cleared the last of the ice at the end of the season. All was set for a clear run home unless they ran into trouble with bad weather or hostile ships. During the Napoleonic wars French corvettes disguised as whale-ships captured and burnt some British ships, but one captain saw through their deception. Seeing the corvette from a distance he realized that the imposter's whaling gear was mounted on the starboard rather than the port side, as was usual, and made his escape into some pack ice.

Even on their arrival home the whale crews were not safe and were subjected to a practice that they bitterly resented. This was the press-gang operated by a navy desperately short of seamen. The higher grades of whalemen, the harpooners and boatsteerers, were exempt from the press provided they could get tickets from the Customs offices. To reach the offices and claim their tickets the men had to resort to subterfuge, dressing as women, being carried in barrels, or arming themselves with harpoons and lances and marching to the Customs in force.

William Scoresby once saved his crew when a revenue cutter bore down on them by opening a tap in the hull that was normally used for filling ballast casks. The ship began to fill with water and the men were set to work the pumps. When the revenue officer came on board Scoresby pointed out that if any of his crew were taken the ship would sink. The officer was not easily fooled. He ordered pumping to cease and checked for himself that the water level started to rise. Satisfied that there really was a leak he returned to his ship. Scoresby turned off the tap, his men pumped the hold dry and the ship reached home safely.

The British Arctic whale fishery did not decline in the same manner as that of the American sperm-whalers. Although disasters such as those of 1835 and 1836 set the industry back it seemed to be more adaptable than the larger New England industry. The British whalers were quicker to use firearms and rapidly saw the advantages of steam. Tug boats had been used regularly to tow the whale-ships out of harbour, but in 1852 Sir Edward Belcher's expedition in search of Franklin used their tug to tow a Dundee whale-ship to the coast of Baffin Island. The Americans did not use tugs in the Arctic until 1882 although Thomas Williams shipped a small steamboat on the deck of his whaler in 1878, using it to chase whales among the floes.

William Penny had plans to convert a whale-ship to steam in 1853, and in 1858 an engine was installed in a Dundee ship. Steam power was only used as an accessory to sail but it took much of the misery out of Arctic navigation. No longer did becalmed ships have to wait helplessly as ice drifted towards them, nor did they have to claw away from rocky shores in the face of the wind. Before the introduction of steam the only way to move a becalmed ship was for the crew to tow it with the boats or 'track' it, by dragging it on foot along the edge of a floe. Now they could admire the view from the deck as they steamed through the ice. The ship could also steam into the wind to go to the assistance of its boats as they laboriously towed their catch. The main danger was that the screw might be broken if it hit a floe.

Another experiment at the same time failed dismally. Iron steamers were built at Hull and Peterhead. Six set out in 1859, two sank after their first contact with ice and the remainder were distinctly unsuccessful. Not for another seventy years could iron-hulled ships compete with tough, resilient wooden hulls for safety in ice.

About the same time as the Americans were turning their attention to right whales in the seas around Greenland, their Pacific fleets were augmenting their catch of sperm whales with Greenland right whales or bowheads. Previously they had been taken in several parts of the Pacific but in 1835 they were discovered in the Kodiak ground off Alaska and in 1843 they were found off Kamchatka. In the following years they were pursued in the

Figure 17 The Arctic whaling grounds.

Okhotsk Sea and in 1848 Captain Royce of the *Superior* passed through the Bering Straits into the Arctic Ocean.

The onslaught on the bowheads became the final upsurge of American whaling. Based mainly on San Francisco and Honolulu the whalers cruised both North and South Pacific. At the start of the voyage they sailed south on the 'between season cruise', hunting sperm whales and breaking in the crews for the bowhead fishing that started as the ice broke up. There was an appalling waste of a rich natural resource in bowhead whaling. Before the stocks became diminished the whalers sometimes took the whalebone only. They reckoned that it was quicker and more profitable to kill another whale than to go to the trouble of cutting-in and trying-out the blubber.

The happy state of the bowhead fishery lasted until 1871, when it was dealt a severe blow similar to the disasters that befell the British fleet in the 1830's. Ships had been lost in the ice every year but in 1871 only seven whale-ships survived out of the fleet of about forty that had sailed north.

As was their habit, the fleet followed the bowheads on their northward migration from the vicinity of Japan into the Bering Sea and then up to the Arctic Ocean. This year they found heavy ice in the Bering Sea and one ship was crushed there. The Bering Straits were finally penetrated in June but there was so much ice that whaling was barely possible and the whalers filled in time by hunting walruses. Only in the final days of July did the ice clear sufficiently for whaling to start in earnest. The fleet worked its way up the coast of Alaska making for Point Barrow on the northernmost tip of Alaska. But on August 29th a strong wind sprang from the south-west and the ice began to close in, forcing the ships towards the shore and trapping them between two headlands near Wainwright Inlet. Thirty-four ships were caught there while a further seven lay at the edge of the pack ice at Icy Cape, some seventy miles to the south.

At first the situation did not seem too desperate as the thick ice floes around the ships were resting on the seabed and it only needed a change of wind to blow them away. But the change never came and tremendous pressure built up in the pack ice so that it was gradually forced over the seabed and on to the shore. The ships could not escape and on September 2nd the first was crushed. Within a week two more were wrecked. In one case the

9

floes suddenly parted and the crushed husk of the ship dropped between them, giving the crew barely time to jump on to the ice.

It was now obvious that there was little chance of the fleet getting clear and a boat was dispatched to Icy Cape to ask the ships there to stand by. On the 14th about 1,200 men, together with the families of several of the captains set out in the boats, abandoning their ships in order to run for those waiting outside the pack. They made the journey in two days, battling through snowstorms and freshly forming ice, but they reached the safety of the waiting ships and all eventually arrived in Honolulu.

The sequel to this disaster that threw several ship-owners out of business was galling in the extreme. Less than two weeks after the ships had been abandoned the long hoped-for north-easterly gale sprang up and cleared the pack ice. But it was too late; only one ship was saved when the whalers returned the following year. The others had sunk, been carried away in the ice or had been burnt by Eskimos.

While hunting bowheads in the northern seas, the whalers sometimes took other species as they presented themselves, such as humpbacks and gray whales. These two also became the object of an intense, but short-lived, fishery that flourished along the coast of Upper and Lower California. It was in 1846 that whalers first came to hunt along these arid shores in the late winter before sailing up to the Arctic. By 1848, fifty ships were taking part in what became known as 'bay-whaling' or 'kelp-whaling'; the season ran from December to February as the whales migrated close to the land.

On arrival at the estuaries and lagoons of California the whale-ships were securely moored, the sails and sailing gear removed and the cutting stage erected. In later years ships were dispensed with, shore stations set up and the whales were cut-in and tried-out on the beach after the manner of the seventeenth century New Englanders, and the Basques before them.

When sufficient numbers of gray whales had congregated in the lagoons the boats were launched in their pursuit. This was the most dangerous whaling of all. The shallow lagoons gave neither boats nor whales much room to manoeuvre and the gray whales were aggressive, earning themselves the name of devil-fish. More powerful than right, and faster than sperm whales, harpooned gray whales careered about the lagoons capsizing boats and entangling whale-lines. The casualties to boats and men were high, as the whales would attack without provocation.

Greener's guns were essential to harpoon these swift creatures and the whalers preferred to harpoon those that were accompanied by calves. They had, of necessity, to swim slowly so it was easier to close with them both for harpooning and delivering the *coup de grâce* with a bomb-lance. Another tactic was for the whalers to lie in wait with their boats in the beds of kelp and shoot the whales as they passed.

In a year or so the whales became wary of the waiting whale-boats and these were replaced by small boats carrying one oarsman and a gunner. This ruse lasted several seasons after which it was impossible to approach the whale without alarming it and it had to be chased until a bomb could be fired into it. When it had slowed down, a harpoon was struck into its body so that when it died and sank the position could be marked with a buoy. About a day later the carcase would rise to the surface and be towed in for flensing. An even more callous method was the harpooning of a calf and dragging it ashore so that the parent could be shot from the beach as it attempted to succour its offspring. A final method, known as 'sailing them down', was to follow and overtake the migrating whales in boats under sail.

Despite the dangers that killed or crippled many a whaler, bay-whaling was extremely popular and was prosecuted with incredible zeal. Ships were lightened and dragged over shoals into the lagoons, where they could easily be endangered by sudden gales, and the harpooners did not stop at striking 'devil-fish'. They also attacked the yet larger and faster blue whales and fin whales, although these rorquals were usually left alone because of the difficulty of catching them and the poor quality of their oil and whalebone.

In 1851 Scammon estimated that a thousand or more gray whales passed down the coast each day. About twenty years later this number had been reduced to forty and early in the twentieth century the Californian gray whale was thought to be extinct. In fact, it had survived in very small numbers and, under strict protection, it is now recovering. By 1961 there were thought to be about 6,000 Californian gray whales and their migration has become a tourist spectacle drawing hundreds of thousands of sightseers each year.

13. The Final Phase

The continual quest for new sources of whales became more urgent at the end of the nineteenth century. The Arctic grounds were almost spent and in the North Atlantic the Norwegians were beginning to hunt rorquals, the only untapped reserve of large whales remaining in the northern hemisphere. In the southern hemisphere there still remained the largest concentration of whales in the world, and in 1892 four Scottish whale-ships left Dundee for the Southern Ocean. Their commission was based on a report by Sir James Clark Ross who had sailed deep into the Weddell Sea in 1844. He wrote:

> We observed a very great number of the largest-sized black (right) whales, so tame that they allowed the ship sometimes almost to touch them before they would get out of the way; so that any number of ships might procure a cargo of oil in a short time. Thus . . . we have discovered . . . a valuable whale-fishery well worth the attention of our enterprising merchants!

Ross was one of the most respected polar explorers so the Dundee whalers had every right to be optimistic as to the outcome of their expedition. But the expedition was a complete failure, they had been forestalled by both British and American whalers who had often turned from sperm-whaling to hunt right whales in polar waters or to catch them as they migrated into warmer waters. The Scotsmen drew a complete blank with right whales and, in desperation, one harpooner struck at a blue whale. The line raced out and that from another boat had to be bent on. This was insufficient and a third boat was brought in. The whale was now towing six lines and three boats and the men managed to get a line to the parent ship, which was added to the procession moving over the sea. Fourteen hours later, the whale's rush had still not abated, so the ship's engines were put astern, and the line snapped.

There must have been considerable gloom on board the four ships as they made their way back up the Atlantic. There were no longer sufficient right whales to support their industry but the expedition had unwittingly missed the chance of establishing a considerable fishery for humpbacks which existed in large numbers around South Georgia, a large island on the fringes of the Southern Ocean. Despite the failure with the blue whale ways had now been found to hunt the faster rorquals and a rorqual fishery was already in existence in the North Atlantic, thanks to the inventiveness and persistence of one man, the Norwegian Svend Føyn, whose work eventually paved the way to the establishment of whaling in the Antarctic.

A sealer by trade, Føyn had long been interested in whaling and had reached the conclusion that the industry could only survive if some way could be found of hunting the rorquals. He spent several years experimenting and finally brought into being the technique that revolutionized whale-hunting.

Svend Føyn's basic invention was a powerful harpoon gun far superior to the Greener's gun and its contemporaries, which were little more than hand-guns mounted in a standard whale-boat. Føyn's gun was a heavy cannon mounted in the bows of a small steam vessel. It fired a large harpoon with an explosive head, that severely wounded or killed the whale, and trailed a five-inch line so that the dead whale could be winched to the surface and filled with compressed air to prevent it from sinking.

Føyn's ship, the *Spes et Fides*, which carried equipment based on several years' experiment, had its first successful cruise in 1868 when he caught thirty whales in Varanger Fjord. At last it was possible to make fast to the largest whales, kill them, prevent them from sinking, then tow them home. And it was all done in comparative safety. One hundred years later harpoon guns and whale-catchers are still recognizable as having evolved from Svend Føyn's prototype, although modern catchers are about five times the gross weight of the *Spes et Fides* and have a maximum speed of eighteen knots. This, then, is a suitable time to describe a modern whale-catcher and its operation.

The original Føyn harpoon guns were muzzle-loaders but these have been replaced by breech-loaders that employ 14 ounces of smokeless powder to propel a 150 lb, six-foot harpoon. When 1eady for firing the harpoon has a grenade containing six ounces of powder screwed to the tip. A time fuse is set to detonate the grenade after the harpoon has entered the whale, crippling or, with luck, killing it. A recent innovation is a saucer-shaped rather than pointed tip to the harpoon head to prevent ricochets and make the harpoon turn downwards if it strikes a glancing blow. Behind the grenade are four barbed flukes that pivot on hinges and fly out after the harpoon is embedded in the whale. Until then, they are tied against the shaft with cord and the whole harpoon is held in the barrel of the gun with more cord. The front section of the shaft, which bears the flukes and grenade, pivots on the main length. While the flukes are tied in place they hold the two sections rigid but after they have flown out the main part of the shaft is free to fold along the whale's back, so reducing the drag and preventing the harpoon head from being pulled out (see Figure 18).

Figure 18 Modern harpoon (a) before firing and (b) after striking the whale, when the grenade has exploded and the flukes have spread.

The three-inch diameter shaft has a slot running most of its length. The slot takes a wire loop to which the whale-line is attached. When the gun is fired, the loop slides to the base of the harpoon shaft and the line follows cleanly, steadying the flight of the harpoon instead of dragging it down.

The gun is mounted on a platform over the bows of the whale-catcher, where there has been a trend to raise the height of the bows almost to a level with the bridge. The two are connected by a catwalk so that the skipper, who is also gunner, can guide the catcher up to the whale, then race down to the gun at the last minute.

The rope attached to the harpoon consists first of a seventy fathom forerunner, once of hemp now of nylon. To this is attached 120-fathom lengths of manilla. When the whale is harpooned the rope is hauled in by a heavy winch mounted just forward of the deckhouse. But even 7½-inch manilla cannot stand the strain of being stretched between a desperate, wounded whale and a whale-catcher bouncing over the waves. The whale has, therefore, to be played, as a game-fish is played on the finest tackle. Line is let out or taken in as the pull on it varies and, to prevent sudden tugs snapping the line, it is passed through the whalers' equivalent of a flexible fishing rod. The line travels from the winch to a sheave half-way up the mast and down to the bows (Figure 19). This sheave is attached to a rope that runs to the

Figure 19 The spring mechanism of a whale-catcher that reduces the tension and cushions shocks in the whale-line.

masthead and down to a series of accumulator springs in the hold. As tension in the whale-line increases the sheave is pulled down, the springs are stretched and the strain on the whale-line decreases. So movements of whale and catcher are continually being buffered by the accumulator springs.

The range of a modern harpoon gun is fifty fathoms at the outside and gunners prefer to shoot when the whale is not more than 20–30 fathoms

(40–60 yards) away. To get within range the catcher has to be brought up to the whale, not an easy job even with the latest in fast catchers. Until 1937 all catchers were steam-powered, a silent form of propulsion that allowed the whalers to stalk their quarry by what the Norwegians call *luse-jag*. Whales are sighted from the crow's nest and a watch is kept to ascertain their course and the frequency with which they blow. The catcher closes with them at full speed then slows down and manoeuvres into position so that it will be just behind the chosen whale as it blows. The gunner then rushes down to his gun and gives final instructions by hand signals. As the whale's back humps out of the water, he sights along the aiming rod above the gun barrel and fires.

When noisy, but more powerful, diesel engines were introduced it was no longer possible to creep up on a whale unawares. Instead, the whales are chased, a technique called *prøyser-jag*. As they become tired they slow down and have to blow more frequently. If chased hard they have to surface every two to three minutes, and in a quarter to half an hour they will have slowed sufficiently for the catcher to close in. Since World War II asdic or sonar equipment has been used to track whales underwater and, as the high frequency pulses emitted by asdic frightens whales, it has been used to assist in the technique of *prøyser-jag*.

If the whale is not killed outright it must be carefully played by the gunner passing instructions to the helmsman and the engineer who controls the winch, until further harpoons can be shot into it. As soon as there is no life left, it is brought alongside and secured by a chain passed around the narrow part of the tail. A hollow lance attached to an airline is thrust deep into its belly and the body cavity inflated. To improve the catcher's efficiency the carcase is released and left to drift while more whales are hunted. Each whale is marked by a flag bearing the catcher's number, a radar reflector and a radio beacon. Eventually the whale is collected by the catcher and towed home with the rest of its catch. When whales are abundant it may stagger in with two carcases on each side and, in later years, special buoy-boats have been employed in towing to relieve the catchers of even this chore.

When Svend Føyn first started operations he hunted only blue whales. As the largest species of whale it gave the greatest yield of oil for a given amount of effort. His success stimulated the formation of other companies, who turned their attention to other species of rorquals. Catching operations, using Føyn harpoon guns, based on simple shore factories, spread around the North Atlantic; from Spitzbergen to Iceland, into the North Pacific and later to all whaling grounds. The moment was now ripe for the rich Antarctic grounds to be opened. The right whales reported by Sir James Clark Ross were rare but the Southern Ocean was still the home of vast populations of rorquals; particularly humpbacks, blue whales and fin whales.

The first man to exploit this potential was the Norwegian Carl Anton Larsen. His first visit to the Antarctic was in search of seals but he saw the possibility of hunting rorquals there. In 1902 he returned to these waters as the captain of the *Antarctic*, the ship carrying Nordenskjöld's Swedish South Polar Expedition. The *Antarctic* was lost and after many adventures the crew and explorers were rescued by an Argentinian gunboat and taken back to Buenos Aires. Here Larsen put forward his plan to set up a whaling factory to process whales caught in the Antarctic. He secured the necessary financial backing and in 1904 three ships of the *Compania Argentina de Pesca* arrived in the cove of Grytviken, at the head of Cumberland Bay in South Georgia.

When Larsen's expedition arrived whales abounded, and his single whale-catcher found sufficient whales, mainly humpbacks, without having to leave Cumberland Bay. As soon as one was caught it was towed back to Grytviken where a factory had been built from materials brought by the other two ships. The factory continued in use with very little change from 1904 to 1963 and its layout and operations were similar to those of shore factories through-out the world. Like the old shore factories of Spitzbergen, a modern whale factory is a production line for dismembering and processing whale carcases, but on a much larger scale than those at Smeerenburg. Motor winches and steam saws serve to make easy the work that had once to be done by man-power and hand tools, and at Grytviken a steady procession of whale car-cases passed through the factory. On an exceptional day thirty fin whales could disappear into the boilers.

The activities of the factory are centred on the plan, a large area just above the shoreline covered with baulks of timber to give a solid working surface. The whale is winched, tail first, up a slipway and on to the plan where, almost before it has come to a standstill, it is attacked by a gang of men known in Norwegian as *flensers*. They are armed with long-handled, razor-sharp knives with which they slice great slits down the length of the whale.

Wires are attached to the blubber and wound in by the winch so that strips are torn off the underlying flesh, with the assistance of the flensers' knives, and the whale is unpeeled like a giantic banana. The remainder of the carcase, known as the *skrot* is turned over and pulled to one side of the plan leaving room for another whale to be drawn up the slipway. While the flensers attack the second whale, the *skrot* of the first is skilfully timmed of its meat and the skeleton dismembered by the meat-cutting men or *lemmers*.

The blubber, meat and bones are processed separately, each receiving treatment that depends largely on the state of the market for different products. In the early days of Antarctic whaling, the whales were so abundant that the carcases were merely stripped of their blubber and discarded. This was an incredible waste of raw material and was soon stopped by economic factors, and by law, the meat and bones then being processed for oil and the residue used as meatmeal and bonemeal. At times there has also been a market for meat extract and, until synthetics were developed, whales supplied large quantities of Vitamin A (7 lb of the vitamin coming from the liver of a fin whale). The hormones insulin and ACTH, used in the treatment of diabetes and arthritis respectively, have also been extracted from whale glands. After the war years there was a market for whalemeat for human consumption in western countries but it never became popular. In Japan, however, whalemeat is used in several forms and it is shipped back to Japan in refrigerator ships.

The success of the modern phase of whaling is due to one invention. In the early twentieth century the process of hydrogenation was discovered and it became possible to turn a liquid oil into a solid, and odourless, fat. Immediately a new market was opened for whale-oil, whose sales had been decreasing since the introduction of petroleum oil. The oil of whalebone whales is a glyceride made of fatty acids and glycerol, like the oil from most animal fats, but unlike the waxy oils of sperm whales. In hydrogenation the oil is 'hardened' or 'saturated' by adding extra hydrogen atoms to each molecule of glyceride to turn it into a solid fat. In this form whale-oil can be used in the manufacture of soap and margarine. Glycerine is a by-product of soap manufacture which has many industrial uses, and other applications of whale-oil products include the manufacture of varnishes, printing ink and cosmetics.

Whale-oil has always been the principal product of whaling, and at

Grytviken and similar stations the whole whale carcase was boiled down for oil. As soon as the sheets of blubber have been stripped off they are drawn to the top of the plan, cut into sections and fed into cookers. At first the cookers were open tanks, little different from the open tryworks used in earlier centuries and these continued to be used at Grytviken until 1955. The blubber is cut up or 'hogged' and thrown into an open tank where it is cooked with steam for 4–6 hours. After cooling the oil is run out to the separator house where it is centrifuged to remove water and any solid residue.

The advantage of open cooking is that it is carried out at low temperature and pressure which prevents decomposition of the oil and results in a high quality product. Nevertheless it is a slow and inefficient method and various forms of pressure cookers are now used to speed up the process at the expense of quality. The original pressure cookers were tall cylinders with a door at the top through which lumps of blubber were thrown on to grids below. Steam was fed in at a pressure of 60–70 lb/sq in for seven hours to drive the oil out of the blubber. On modern pelagic factories (see p. 140) a rotary Kvaener or Hartmann cooker is used. These are horizontal cookers containing a rotating drum with baffles which break up the blubber and facilitate the removal of oil. The process takes only 2–4 hours and can be operated continuously, but the oil is of a lower quality.

Meanwhile, on the other side of the plan, the bones are being dragged up a slipway to a large steam saw which cuts them into manageable pieces, to be dropped into a pressure cooker where they are cooked at 60–70 lb sq in for twenty hours to express a high quality oil. The solid residue is ground up as bonemeal. The meat, which is also rich in oil receives a different treatment. After hogging, it is passed down a heated tube by means of a rotary screw where it is cooked sufficiently to make it firm. Liquid is squeezed out in a press and centrifuged, first to remove solids which are put back with the meat and again to remove the oil. The remaining liquid, called 'glue-water' contains dissolved proteins and is put back with the meat, together with glue-water from the blubber and bones. The resulting sodden mass is passed through a drier and some of the dissolved proteins from the glue-water go back into the meat which is dried and milled into meatmeal.

All that now remains on the plan are the internal organs. Depending on the circumstances these may be jettisoned or cooked to yield a poor oil and the whalebone is still collected for making brooms.

A modern whale factory working at full pressure to extract as much from each carcase as efficiently as possible calls for careful management. This is particularly important now that shortage of whales and competition from vegetable oils have cut down the margin of profit. The schedule of the factory has to be organized to fit with the arrival of whales at the slipway so that fuel, which has to be transported a long way to the Antarctic, is not wasted. On the other hand whales cannot be allowed to pile up, as the oil in the meat and bones starts to decompose soon after death. If possible, the whale is processed within twenty-four hours of death but the legal maximum is thirty-three hours. If the meat is going to be used for human consumption, the whale must be cut up earlier, or the catcher crew must slit open the body immediately after death to let the sea cool the body and prevent bacterial decomposition. Antibiotics are also pumped into the carcase to prevent spoilage. Large quantities are needed, but they prevent the meat from decaying and preserve the blubber so that a high quality oil is produced.

Since 1965 shore factories have ceased to operate in the Antarctic. They have been superseded by floating factories, which are large ships fitted out to process whales in the manner of shore factories. The first Antarctic floating factory, the *Admiralen*, arrived in southern waters in 1905, only a year after Larsen had started work at Grytviken. The *Admiralen* and its contemporaries operated in sheltered bays, such as the deep bays of South Georgia, or in the flooded volcanic crater of Deception Island in the South Shetlands. The whales were cut up alongside the ship and the pieces hauled in, a method reminiscent of the old days of whaling – and just as hazardous in bad weather.

In 1920 one of these floating factories started work along the ice edge, where the whales congregate, instead of anchoring in a sheltered bay. Its example led the way to the development of pelagic factories, which were floating factories designed for use at sea. They were able to process whales and refuel and service their fleet of catchers far from land.

Two considerations led to the development of pelagic whaling, as this mobile form of operation came to be known. First, it enabled the whalers to hunt among concentrations of whales far from the coastal waters where stocks were already diminishing. To this end, Larsen returned to the Antarctic in command of the pelagic factory *Sir James Clark Ross* to hunt whales in among the ice of the sea that bears Ross' name. The second reason was to avoid control by the British Government.

The shore factories and shore-based floating factories operated in the island groups of the South Shetlands and South Orkneys, along the western coast of Grahamland (now the Antarctic Peninsula), as well as in South Georgia. These all fell into the region of the British Empire known as the Falkland Islands Dependencies, and as soon as the factory at Grytviken started work the British Government stepped in to demand rent and royalties. Larsen's company had to pay export duty on each barrel of oil and £250 a year for the lease of the ground on which their factory stood. The British also insisted on certain restrictions designed to control the exploitation of the whale stocks. Each company was allowed to operate only a specified number of catchers and they had to avoid killing females accompanied by calves. As much as possible of each carcase had to be utilized, and at the shore factories this meant the entire carcase.

Outside territorial waters these rules did not apply so 'pirate' whaling companies started to operate with pelagic factories, with established companies following suit as the method proved successful. In 1925, a new kind of factory ship appeared. The *Lancing* had a slipway running through the stern to the main deck which was fitted out as a flensing plan. Whale carcases were brought up to the slipway and seized around the tail flukes by a massive 'Gjeldstad claw' that closed like a pair of tongs and dragged the whale on to the deck. More factory ships of this pattern followed and, with the stern slipway, and side-by-side funnels leaving room for the whales to be dragged along the centre of the ship, they are as unmistakable as the oldtime whaleship with its brick tryworks. They represent the peak of whaling efficiency, cruising in search of whales, guiding their fleet of catchers by radio as reports of schools of whales come in, processing the whales as efficiently as is possible, transferring the products to transport ships, taking on fuel oil from tankers and bunkering the catchers.

Antarctic whaling became a bonanza in the first decades of this century. The Grytviken company was making good profits by its second year and new companies hastened southwards, but modern whaling is no more independent of economic and international events than was the Yankee sperm-whaling described in earlier chapters. By 1911 there were eight companies in the field and in 1931 forty-one pelagic factories were operating and 40,201 whales were killed, compared with a hundred and ninety-five in 1904. The result was massive overproduction and a glut of whale-oil. The following year most of the factories were laid up and only seven whaling expeditions went south to the Antarctic. At the same time whaling companies voluntarily agreed to restrict the number of whales killed; not to prevent over-killing and a running-down of the stocks, but to avoid overproduction.

After this setback, production crept up again and in 1938 46,039 whales were killed in the Antarctic. World War II then intervened and only one pelagic factory remained in operation. Most of the others were destroyed, their slow speed making them the lame ducks of the convoy system. After the war there was a great demand for edible animal fats, which the whale industry could supply in the form of hardened whale-oil. The whale stocks had partly recovered during the war years but, despite the braking effect of the International Whaling Commission which was set up in 1946, there has been gross over-hunting and Antarctic whaling has gone into decline. Of the two nations that once dominated the scene, the British have given up completely and the Norwegians are now operating on only a very small scale after being dormant for several years. The Southern Ocean is left to comparative newcomers, the Japanese and Russians. The sad story of the drastic decline of the whale stocks and the, unfortunately futile, attempts at stemming the steady drain of some species is told in the next chapter.

Throughout this narrative emphasis has been placed on the main branches of the whaling industry: the right-whaling of Spitzbergen, Yankee sperm-whaling, the Arctic bowhead fishery and Antarctic rorqual whaling. While these are the most important stages in the history of whaling it must not be forgotten that lesser enterprises have been continuing all the time, some of which have been described in Chapter 8. In the present century whaling has come to mean the hunting of whales in Antarctic waters as described in this chapter, but at the beginning of the century a few Biscayan right whales were still being killed each year off British coasts and in 1912 Robert Cushman Murphy sailed in the brig *Daisy* on a sperm-whaling voyage, two centuries after Christopher Hussey had killed his first sperm whale.

As whaling flourished in the Antarctic so did whaling in other parts of the world. Shore factories still operate in Iceland, Norway, South Africa and South America. In the North Pacific pelagic fleets are now catching as many whales as the diminished Antarctic expeditions, but as the numbers of the large rorqual species get nearer to the level of extinction, the attention of whalers has turned to smaller species and sperm whales are again being hunted in large numbers.

The smaller whales and dolphins have always been hunted, and not only by local hunters like the Faeroese and Eskimos. In the latter part of the nineteenth century belugas were hunted extensively off Spitzbergen. Now, however, the refined techniques of modern whaling are bringing increased pressure to bear on the small whales and it is becoming worthwhile to catch whales that were once not worth the cost of chasing.

When the catches of Antarctic fin whales declined drastically in the 1960's, the whalers turned their attention to the smaller sei whales, which previously had been ignored because of their small size and poor oil yield. The very similar Bryde's whale is also caught off South Africa and in the North Atlantic the Norwegians prosecute a vigorous fishery for small whales which yield little oil and are caught for their meat. Some 3,000–5,000 whales are caught each year in a season that lasts from March to September. They are harpooned from fishing boats and the catch includes minke, killer and pilot whales. Large numbers of minkes and pilot whales are harpooned or driven ashore off Newfoundland, where one of their uses is as food for ranch mink.

The problem of the small whale fishery is that it is exempt from the regulations that cover the catching of the large whales. As a result the stocks of small whales are being steadily drained. The minke whale is under particular pressure as it migrates up the Norwegian coast and gathers to feed in the Barents Sea. Unfortunately, females with young are the first on the scene and come closest inshore. The history of whaling legislation is described in the next chapter and it is almost wholly concerned with the protection of the largest whales. The smaller whales, dolphins and porpoises are not covered by even the limited safeguards given to their larger relatives.

14. Legislation and Conservation

Control of the whaling industry is not a new idea, but until the present century legislation consisted of those in power attempting to procure as large a share of the catch as possible. Only when the shares looked as if they were going to disappear was any attempt made to protect the whales. Mediaeval rulers issued laws that claimed stranded whales for their own, acts as selfish as that of demanding treasure-trove. Later, when whaling became an industry, governments tried to assert monopolies over the whaling-grounds. Ownership of the Spitzbergen whaling-grounds was a source of dispute for many years and in 1821 the Russian Government tried to exclude foreign whalers from the Bering Sea.

In 1904 the first law preventing the killing of whales was passed. Whaling was banned along the Norwegian coast for the rather bizarre reason that the fishermen believed that fin whales were intimately concerned with the arrival of the herring shoals and a decline in the herring catch led to the 'Menhavn riots'. The Norwegian whalers had to shift their operations to British waters, where they ran into the same trouble.

About this time the Antarctic whaling industry was becoming established and, until the development of pelagic floating factories, all operations were based at stations leased from the Falkland Islands Government. The whaling companies were expected to observe a set of rules that attempted to rationalize the industry and prevent over-exploitation of the whale stocks. Each company was limited in the number of catchers it could employ and the maximum amount of each carcase had to be utilized. The gunners were also to avoid harpooning female whales which were accompanied by calves.

The coming of pelagic factories rendered these regulations valueless and whaling in the Antarctic proceeded unchecked. In 1925, when the *Lancing* made her first voyage, the total Antarctic catch was 10,488 whales. By 1931 it had risen to 40,201 and a consequent glut of whale-oil led the companies to cut down their operations and save themselves from liquidation. The number of floating factories was reduced from forty-seven to seven and the world catch was reduced by over one-quarter during the following year. In succeeding years, however, the catch increased and in 1935 regulations to cut the size of the catch were introduced under the auspices of the League of Nations and in 1937 most whaling nations signed the International Whaling Agreement. These were the first attempts at whaling legislation to be aimed at preservation of whales on an international scale.

The League of Nations regulations formed the basis of subsequent controls on the whaling industry and, like the industry itself, they were concerned primarily with the Antarctic populations of whales. Limits were imposed on the movements of floating factories and the catching of undersize whales was forbidden. The latter rule was designed to eliminate the catching of immature animals, a wasteful act which was very damaging to the whale populations. The size limits were set at seventy feet for blue whales and fifty-five feet for fin whales. At the same time the Agreement banned the catching of gray whales and right whales. In 1938 Antarctic humpbacks were also given protection and part of the Southern Ocean was set aside as a sanctuary. Inspectors were appointed to each factory to ensure that the regulations were not flouted.

During World War II little whaling was undertaken and in 1946 the industry started again almost from scratch. An International Whaling Commission was established by the interested nations to work out and administer regulations for the conservation of whale stocks, and thus of the whaling industry as well. It has a scientific sub-committee to collect biological information on the whales and advise on measures to be taken for their preservation. The Commission deliberates on the scientists' recommendations and advises the member governments accordingly. The latter can disagree and opt out of any decisions that the Commission has made.

International bodies for controlling the exploitation of resources are rare, and doubly so when the resource is in international waters, as with whales. The International Whaling Commission is a remarkable body with quite unusual powers, in that measures can be agreed upon by nations with admirable speed. It has great achievements to its credit but it cannot be denied that there are shortcomings in its organization. The members of the Commission

10

do not always agree on every step to be taken and their decisions are not binding on the governments involved.

Critics of the Commission point out that, although it has arranged for the number of whales killed each year to be cut down and it has obtained protection for the seriously endangered species, these steps have generally come too late. There are some interested observers who claim that the Commission, far from preserving whale stocks, is presiding over their extinction. These criticisms are largely valid; but the limitations of the Commission's power have to be appreciated. The scientific advisers cannot force their views on the whaling nations and their arguments are seriously undermined by the lack of knowledge about whale biology. As we have seen in the first part of this book, it has not been easy to make estimates of longevity, birthrate and other factors that make it possible to assess the size of whale populations.

Under natural conditions an animal population produces surplus offspring to compensate for those animals lost through predation, disease or accident, and so keeps the population level. If the population is suddenly affected by an outbreak of disease, or by hunting, the loss can be compensated to a greater or lesser extent by increasing the surplus through a higher birthrate, increased survival of young animals, or decreased age of maturity. This surplus can be removed from the population without the total numbers dropping and is the sustainable yield that man can crop from an animal population. In other words, it is the interest on which he can live without touching the capital.

The size of the sustainable yield has been the elusive goal of whale conservationists and in the absence of firm scientific data it has not been possible to assess it accurately, and so obtain effective limits for the numbers killed by the whaling industry. In 1970 there was still no agreement on the sustainable yield for the Antarctic fin whales; the population of whales that has been studied in the greatest detail.

The story of the attempt to limit whaling is depressing; it is a case of shutting a succession of doors after the horse has bolted. In 1944 an agreement was made to limit the numbers of whales killed each year in the Antarctic. A figure was set at two-thirds of the pre-war catch and divided between the participating nations. The size of the catch is calculated in blue whale units (BWU), or the number of blue whales and equivalents in other species. One blue whale is reckoned to be the equivalent of two fin whales, two and a half humpbacks or six sei whales. In the first year of post-war whaling the quota was set at 16,000 BWU and was made up of a combination of blue whales, fin whales and sei whales.

This method of limiting the catch has an intrinsic drawback in that it gives an overall limit of the numbers of whales caught but no limit for the number from individual species. The result was that each species in turn was attacked until it became rare. The blue whale was the largest and the most profitable species to pursue. Its numbers had already shown a decrease before the war, but after the war it was attacked again and it became rare by 1955. As the blue whale became increasingly difficult to find the whalers turned their attention to the fin whale. To achieve the annual quota twice as many fin whales had to be killed as the equivalent blue whales and their numbers dropped rapidly in the early 1960's (Figure 20). Then the comparatively small sei whale, which

Figure 20 World catch of blue, fin and sei whales. There was a general increase in hunting after World War II. Blue whales soon went into decline and the fin whale catch soared. When the numbers of fin whales dropped, sei whales were caught in increasing numbers.

was once shunned as being unprofitable, was hunted and it, too, soon showed signs of being overhunted. The smaller whales – bottlenose, killer, beaked and minke – are already being hunted in some parts of the world, and pressure on them will no doubt grow.

The post-war overhunting of blue, fin and sei whales has occurred despite the International Whaling Commission frequently revising the annual Antarctic quota, bringing it down in stages from 16,000 BWU in 1952 to 2,700 in 1970. Cuts in the quota could only be imposed when the whalers felt that numbers had already decreased so far that they would be unable to catch many more whales without a restriction being in force, and the failure of the quota system to halt the decline of the whale stocks is shown by the inability of the whaling fleets to catch even the reduced quotas of later years. In 1969 the quota of 2,700 BWU was not reached and the Antarctic fleets (three Japanese factories, three Russian and one Norwegian) caught only 2,477 BWU (3,000 fin whales and 5,856 sei whales) between them. In modern times sperm whales have been largely ignored but they are now caught in increasing numbers, particularly in the northern Pacific, which is now replacing the Antarctic as the main whaling ground.

When the whaling industry as a whole has deliberately reduced its raw material to a level where it cannot fulfil its own objectives, the inability of the International Whaling Commission to ensure that all the rules governing the protection of whales are observed seems insignificant. However, there is no doubt that a blind eye is often turned at the factories when a member of a protected species is brought in or if a crooked measurement puts an undersized whale over the legal minimum length.

There was no great cause for alarm when the Antarctic whales first showed signs of diminishing, because it was felt by many whalers that the time would eventually come when there would be too few whales for whaling to pay. As whaling was an expensive business, it was thought this would happen before the stocks diminished too far. But the Antarctic whales have virtually disappeared without whaling ceasing. It is possible to sail through the Southern Ocean without seeing a whale and Ross' account of their abundance quoted in Chapter 13 seems fantastic.

The fact that whaling has not ceased is due to two factors. First, whale products are very valuable, even in the face of competition from fish and vegetable materials. It is therefore worth mounting expeditions to hunt the few remaining whales. If necessary, the industry can be bolstered with subsidies. Furthermore, a whaling fleet represents a considerable investment in capital; and one cannot be easily laid-up. Whaling operations have, in consequence, been forced to continue and this has been made possible by increased technical efficiency. The catcher boats have increased in size and power; the whales are killed with less effort; there are improved methods of finding the whales; and a better use is made of the carcasses. Despite such efficiency, the boats are chasing fewer whales with diminishing reward; but there is little sign of a let-up in their activity.

It is exasperating to read the reports of the International Whaling Commission over the last two decades. The scientists of the Commission have managed to amass and analyse a vast body of information on the biology of whales and statistics collected from the whaling companies give the numbers of each species killed in every year. But the bald statements of the reports show the inability of the whaling nations to agree with the scientists' evidence and reduce the quotas to levels whereby the whale populations will get a chance to recover. On some occasions nations have left the Commission rather than agree to proposals that would damage their interests. It seems that each country wants to play an equally large part in the killing of the goose that lays the golden eggs.

The futility of their actions are shown to the full by figures presented by Dr Mackintosh, one time Director of Research of the Discovery Committee, and an expert on whale populations. Dr Mackintosh has shown the extent of the decrease in Antarctic whale stocks. They started to fall in the 1950's and really slumped in the 1960's. He has also shown what would have been the effect of a total ban on whaling at various times in the recent past. If fin whales had been protected in 1960 their numbers would have recovered sufficiently to give a maximum sustainable yield of 20,000 per year by about 1970 (Figure 21). This means that just a few years idleness by the whaling fleets, or a few more years on a very restricted quota, would have allowed them to revert to pre-war catches. By 1968 the situation had worsened so that a ban would have to be imposed until the early 1980's to have a similar effect.

The blue whale has suffered more than the fin whale. It was diminishing sharply before the war and by 1963 its estimated population was in the order of one thousand. Only in 1965 was it given complete protection, but its survival now seems ensured, although it will take perhaps a century to recover completely. The Antarctic catch of rorquals is now made up of fin whales and sei whales, and some authorities on whale stocks optimistically consider that,

Figure 21 Trends in the population of Antarctic fin whales, after World War II. (a) projected increase if whaling ceased in 1960, (b) projected increase if stopped in 1968. A population of 150,000 would give a sustainable yield of 20,000 (modified from Mackintosh).

because the annual quota has been below the sustainable yield for the remaining stocks of both species since 1967, they now have the chance to recover. The inability of the whalers to catch even their allotted quota in recent years has led to a running-down of the whaling fleets which may further increase the chances of recovery.

The western world, at least, is becoming conservation-minded but it is still difficult to show concrete examples of a radical change of attitude towards conservation problems by the people with power to act, even when these problems concern our daily lives. The fate of the whales is far from home; until recently it received little publicity and made no impact, so it has not been on the public conscience. Then in June 1972, the UN Conference on the Human Environment recommended a ten-year ban on whaling. This received considerable publicity but, at the International Whaling Commission meeting shortly afterwards the ban was rejected. On the other hand, whaling had now become the subject of public discussion.

Public crusades have not saved seal pups, for instance, despite the emotional appeal they arouse. The trade in sealskins continues in the face of a large press coverage and representations to the governments concerned. Even if there were a campaign for the protection of whales it would suffer from the lack of an eyecatching piece of propaganda on which to focus the public's attention. The photograph of a sealer with club poised over a baby seal is far more emotive than the equivalent picture of a whaler training a harpoon gun at the dimly-seen back of a whale. A campaign against the use of the products of whaling would be equally ineffective because they are not easily identified despite being all around us: margarine, soap, suntan oil, paint, shoe polish and pet food to name a few. Pressure has been brought to bear on the manufacturers of pet food to stop using whale meat, but they use only a small fraction of the available product, so this is unlikely to influence the whaling companies.

The 1972 meeting of the International Whaling Commission may well have been the turning point for the whaling industry and the whales. The publicity received by the call for the ban on whaling at the UN Conference, and its rejection by the Commission, obscured the real achievements of the Commission. After many years of argument, it had managed to start an International Observer Scheme, whereby nations will exchange observers to report on each others' whaling activities. Furthermore, the system of allotting quotas was overhauled. The Blue Whale Unit has been dropped in favour of separate quotas for each species. Quotas for sperm, sei and minke whales have been set at levels which will prevent overexploitation, and the quota for fin whales (1,950 in the Antarctic) will allow numbers to increase. There are still some deficiencies to be made good: some whaling nations do not belong to the Commission and do not follow its rules, and there is no protection for small whales and dolphins. But it does seem that the great whales have been saved. The main problem now is whether it is ethical to kill these animals at all, but that is a problem that extends well beyond the subject of whaling.

Further Reading

A number of the old whaling books are being republished. They make fascinating reading to anyone interested in sailing ships or adventure stories. All books on whale biology necessarily cover much the same ground but this short list gives the most useful works, from which the eager student can progress.

WHALING

The Cruise of the Cachalot, Frank T. Bullen. John Murray, London.
Moby Dick, Herman Melville. J. M. Dent, London.
Old Whaling Days, Captain W. Barron. Conway Maritime Press.
Logbook for Grace, Robert Cushman Murphy. Robert Hale, London.
South Latitude, F. D. Ommaney. Longmans, London.

WHALES

The Stocks of Whales, N. A. Mackintosh. Fishing News (Books) Ltd.
Whales, E. J. Slijper. Hutchinson, London.

GENERAL

The Whale, ed. L. Harrison Matthews. George Allen & Unwin, London.
Lost Leviathan, F. D. Ommaney. Hutchinson, London.
Marine Mammals, Charles M. Scammon. Dover, New York.

Index

Pilot Whale

Killer Whale

Fin Whale

Blue Whale

Bryde's Whale

Baird's Beaked Whale

Sperm Whale

Grey Whale

Pigmy Right Whale